The
BULL TERRIER

EDITED BY
DAVID HARRIS

BEST of BREED

ACKNOWLEDGEMENTS

The publishers would like to thank the following for help with photography: John and Mandy Young (Bullyview); Dawn Godsall (Neverland); Brian Smalley (Briden); Malcolm Presland (Kofyn); Hearing Dogs for Deaf People and Pets As Therapy. A very special thank you to Alice van Kempen for her stunning photos of Bull Terriers.

Cover photo: © Tracy Morgan Animal Photography (www.animalphotographer.co.uk)
pages 2, 3, 6, 18, 46, 60, 78, 106 and 128 © Alice van Kempen
pages 104 and 105 reproduced by kind permission of Louis B. Ruediger.
pages 17 and 35 © Alan V. Walker; page 50 © istockphoto.com/Griselda Amorim

The British Breed Standard reproduced in Chapter 7 is the copyright of the Kennel Club and published with the club's kind permission. Extracts from the American Breed Standard are reproduced by kind permission of the American Kennel Club.

THE QUESTION OF GENDER
The 'he' pronoun is used throughout this book instead of the rather impersonal 'it', but no gender bias is intended.

First published in 2009 by The Pet Book Publishing Company Limited
Chepstow, NP16 7LG, UK.

This edition printed 2010. Reprinted in 2013.

ISBN
978-1-906305-17-8
1-906305-17-X

Printed and bound in China through Printworks International Ltd.

CONTENTS

GETTING TO KNOW BULL TERRIERS

Chapter 1

A Bull Terrier is no ordinary dog. The Kennel Club Breed Standard, the blueprint for the breed, describes the Bull Terrier as strongly built, muscular, well balanced and active with a keen, determined and intelligent expression. The head is like no other, egg shaped and solid with mischievous, triangular, deep-set eyes. This ovoid head is set on to a thick, muscular, powerful neck that flows into an equally powerful, muscular body.

The muscle power of a Bull Terrier is exceptional. It is so explosive that they are used to outcross with Lurchers to give the Lurchers an overdrive facility. If a Bull Terrier were to take human form, he would be a bouncer at a nightclub – not belligerent, but more than capable of taking care of himself. The look says it all: "Don't mess with me, mate."

WHAT SIZE IS A BULLY?

The Breed Standard provides a written description of what a Bull Terrier should look like, but there is no guidance as to his size. The Standard states that there are neither weight nor height limits, but there should be the impression of size consistent with quality and sex. It is, however, one of the few Standards that calls for dogs to look masculine and bitches feminine. That still leaves the quandary about size: from a Pug to a Great Dane?

Back in the 1970s, a Bull Terrier stalwart wrote in her critique that she was passed by the Kennel Club to award Challenge Certificates in Bull Terriers not Great Danes, as she considered this particular exhibit too tall! If the Miniature Bull Terrier is restricted by an ideal height not exceeding 35.5 cms (14 ins) then we may assume that somewhere around that baseline and upwards is the required dimension. In general it is safe to say that most Bull Terriers will be taller than a Staffordshire Bull Terrier's 36-41 cms (14-16 ins) and no higher than a Border Collie's 53 cms (21 ins), so therefore we have a dog of medium height.

The weight, however, is a different matter. A strongly-built muscular male will weigh approximately 30 kgs (66 lbs), with a slightly smaller bitch, who, despite her musculature, should still be essentially feminine, tipping the scales at around 26 kgs (57 lbs). So this is not the ideal choice for those of frail physique or nervous disposition.

THE CANINE GLADIATOR

The old blueprint Breed Standard described the Bull Terrier as the "gladiator of the canine race", which, with a modern

This is a powerful, muscular breed, but quality is all important.   *Photo: Alice van Kempen.*

interpretation, does not really convey an accurate picture of the Bull Terrier. The development of the breed from the old Bull and Terrier of the 19th century, due largely to the clever breeding programme and entrepreneurial skills of Birmingham's James Hinks, may well be the basis for this description.

In the late 19th century, when the Bull Terrier was beginning to cause a stir among terrier fanciers, not only was the breed appreciated for its looks, a Bully was expected to fulfil his role when pitted against the similar shorter-faced variety that has become the Staffordshire Bull Terrier. Tales abound of dogs and bitches winning glory in the

show ring and then repeating their victory in the fighting pit. These dogs were tough characters, as were their owners, living in extremely harsh circumstances. They were housed in kennels and were literally fighting for their keep. This heritage should never be forgotten. Nowadays the look of the Bull Terrier is usually enough – they are seldom aggressive towards other dogs unless provoked – but the ability to take on all-comers is still there. The description of "full of fire" and "courageous" depicts this belligerent ancestry and is forgotten at one's peril.

The down-faced, egg-shaped head can prove intimidating to

other dogs and humans, particularly with the deep-set, triangular eyes that give a piercing look capable of melting concrete. A Bull Terrier should not be soft and cuddly! A potential purchaser came to see a litter and was shown the puppies' sire, a fine upstanding Bully on his best behaviour. On seeing the sheer size and power of the dog, the potential purchaser visibly blanched, saying he did not realise Bull Terriers "were that big", so I tactfully suggested that a smaller, less powerful breed might be more to his taste.

The sheer size and power of a Bully makes the need for firm handling from an early stage essential. An adult Bully is perfectly capable of towing an adult owner up hill and down dale at an amazing speed for their bulk. Because of this strength, toys for Bull Terriers must be robust – a Bully's idea of heaven is swinging off a suspended tyre. If you give a ball as a plaything, it should be solid, hard rubber of sufficient diameter not to be swallowed and capable of remaining intact despite the power of the Bully's jaws. Soft squeaky toys will be demolished and probably consumed in less time than it has taken to remove the packaging.

All dogs, especially Bullies, will go through the spotty teenage stage where they think they can be 'top dog' and you, the owner, will do their bidding. All pups should be able to be handled by anyone. Your veterinary surgeon will be less than impressed with an out-of-control pup attempting to chew everything and everyone when presented for his first vaccination. You must be able to check your pup's ears, eyes and feet and cut their nails from the earliest age or by the time your cute pup has matured into adulthood. Without any form of discipline he will be a liability and a danger, which could cost him his life.

COLOURS

If you asked a member of the general public what colour is a Bull Terrier, back would come the reply, "White", often mentioning their pink eyes. In fact, this is a popular misconception, as a Bull Terrier has dark brown eyes, but with pink eye rims on an all-white head.

The original white Bull Terrier owned by James Hinks has altered little in its colour pattern. It is allowable, and some think desirable, to have head markings, which may be a small or large eye patch or patches, with partially coloured ears or solid-coloured ears. There may be additional head markings but none should extend behind the collar.

If there is truth in the allegation that James Hinks used Dalmatian in the mix to produce his ideal Bull Terrier, the heavily ticked puppy coats may be attributable to this, as can the heavily pigmented skin sometimes visible through moulting coats. Ticking with coloured hairs after adulthood should be considered a fault.

Pigmentation in the white Bull Terrier can be a problem. Most pups are born with pink noses that colour up as they mature to the desired blackness. Eye rims, if heavily pigmented in an all-white head, will have the effect of making the eye look larger and the expression softer. There have been several mismarked Champions over the years, with patches on the rump or tail base; a dog with such a handicap will have to be exceptional elsewhere if it is to win in a show ring.

Coloured Bull Terriers come in a variety of hues, the more common being either black, black brindle, brindle, red or fawn, with a large white collar, white blaze down the face and white feet/legs. The coloured area

The typical Bull Terrier head, with a piercing look from deep-set, triangular eyes, can prove to be daunting. *Photo: Alice van Kempen.*

BULL TERRIER COLOURS

The popular belief is that the Bull Terrier is an all-white dog.
Photo: Alice van Kempen.

The red Bull Terrier often has a large white collar.
Photo: Alice van Kempen.

on the back and possibly including head markings are rather like a tuxedo jacket – hence a further similarity to the bouncers on the door. Often names reflect this coat pattern, Jack Mildenhall's Ch. Hollyfir's Dog in a Doublet being a prime example.

It is also possible to have a tri-colour Bull Terrier. Here, again, the dinner jacket coat pattern is the aim. Blue or liver coats are highly undesirable and seldom occur. In the acceptable colours, you may encounter solid colours with no white markings, which gives the Bull Terrier an almost prehistoric look. Solid black brindles have

always reminded me of dinosaurs.

In reds and fawns there is usually darker black shading around the eyes and muzzle and edging the facial blaze; this does emphasise the markings on the head. Many coloured Bull Terriers will appear to have a round, bold eye compared to the white variety, but usually this is the dark pigmentation around the eye creating this undesirable illusion. Similarly, uneven markings, such as a white left foot with a solid white right leg, will look odd when the dog is moving, as the eye tends to be drawn to the white leg approaching. Even marking is the aim of every

coloured Bull Terrier breeder; it seems that a white Bully with a patch on his rump is mismarked when his coloured cousin may get away with a large white patch on his back and not be considered mismarked.

There have been several Bull Terriers in the past few years that have been marked more like a Friesian cow than a Bull Terrier and it is hard to decide if they are heavily mismarked white Bull Terriers or extremely badly marked coloured Bull Terriers. There is yet to be mentioned a Harlequin in the colours allowed; this is the prerogative of the Great Dane and should stay so.

The flashy markings of a brindled Bull Terrier.
Photo: Alice van Kempen.

A tri-coloured Bull Terrier.
Photo: Alice van Kempen.

DEAFNESS

Unfortunately, it is fairly common to encounter deafness in Bull Terriers, the main culprits being the white variety but the coloured versions are not immune to this defect. If constantly breeding white to white for too many generations, there is a strong possibility of increasing the chances of deafness, and also the white coat will lose its brightness. Most current breeders will have their pups checked for deafness with a Baer test and it is not unreasonable to expect any intended purchase to have been tested (see Chapter 3: A Bull Terrier for your Lifestyle).

Deaf dogs are trainable, *but* there is always the risk that they could run out of sight of the hand signals and cause mayhem on a road, for which the owner is legally liable.

Bully pups love to play, but watch out for the needle-sharp teeth...

CLOWN DOGS

As young pups Bull Terriers closely resemble piglets, particularly in their stiff-legged bouncing movement. They are natural clowns and love to entertain.

You may be drawn into complicity with a puppy's playfulness – but forget the sharpness of puppy teeth at your peril. There are those who suggest that these 'clowns' are merely exploring with their teeth for want of hands. However, the parent of a small toddler may regard this 'exploration' with a slightly less rose-tinted glow.

Though alluring, playful and, indeed, great fun, this 'clowning' should be within the owner's delineated bounds of acceptability in order to avoid 'the tears of the clown'.

A stout pair of Wellington boots are a useful addition to your outfit when pegging out washing accompanied by a boisterous Bull Terrier pup intent on chewing your ankle bones. Washing itself holds a fascination for Bull Terriers, who are unable to resist the joy of swinging off the washing on the line (not much washing will support the weight of a fully grown Bull

Terrier). For pups, unwashed washing is equally irresistible; socks, pants and favourite sweaters are regarded as a readily available source of fibre to aid digestion!

Adult Bull Terriers do have the ability to soft pedal round the very young or infirm. They seem to understand that their normal 'bull in a china shop' approach – a favourite ploy is crashing into the back of one's knees at high speed – may well cause injury and/or rebuke, and is best saved for those who can withstand such onslaught.

NANNY DOGS

Most Bull Terrier bitches are quite maternal and will gravitate towards a young child or baby, particularly if they themselves have had pups. I have even seen a bitch with a litter refuse to settle until the visiting baby was included in her litter – this is, however, not a recommended procedure.

Somewhere in a cupboard, gathering dust no doubt, is a photo of one bitch in the paddling pool with my children when they were little more than toddlers, quite content to act as nanny. Yet this self-same bitch would happily warn off any stranger approaching us in the park, and, when having her obligatory mad half-hour of chasing round the garden, would flatten anyone in her path.

AN IDEAL HOME

A medium to large garden is essential for the sudden mad

KENNEL DOGS

Bull Terriers can live as kennel dogs, but take care with the type of bedding you provide, as it will frequently be devoured. Kennel runs should be large enough to ensure adequate room to play, run and jump. Were you to ask your Bull Terrier, I am sure he would prefer his accommodation to be a comfy chair in front of the fire and to be a part of the family to whom he will give his undying devotion.

This is a breed that seems to gravitate towards small children.

Photo: Alice van Kempen.

bursts of energy when a Bull Terrier pretends to be a Greyhound and tears around at full speed. Walls, steps and ornamental ponds are not advisable. Trees for shade are desirable, but they need to be well established before the acquisition of a Bull Terrier. A young tree will soon be gnawed off at ground level and then brought into the house for approval!

Trying to contain the youthful enthusiasm of a Bull Terrier in a flat is a recipe for disaster. If a Bully is left on his own, he will, as most terriers do, devise his own method of entertainment –

eating houseplants, re-designing kitchens or removing floor tiles. If you have to leave a Bull Terrier alone for any period of time, robust toys will prevent household destruction.

The use of indoor crates has become popular for containing a growing pup to ensure valuables are not chewed, but, as with any dog, a crate should be used appropriately. Any animal imprisoned for long periods of time will go stir-crazy, and boredom in Bull Terriers can lead to tail chasing. Pups of any breed will find their tail to be a thing of wonder and joy, but when Bullies are laughed at when chasing their

appendage, they deem this as approval and consequently repeat *ad nauseum* until it becomes obsessive. Distraction to prevent this is vital, as a confirmed tail chaser will not thrive and eventually will pursue his hobby 24 hours a day to the exclusion of everything else.

Any dog showing concern at his own rear should first be wormed, as worms can cause irritation, which could lead to tail chasing, as could infected anal glands. Thus, if the Bully persists in his attention, a trip to the vet to have the anal glands checked could prevent further trouble. Persistent tail chasers have been

The Bull Terrier needs an outlet for his mad bursts of energy.

known, with dogged determination, to actually catch their own tail (no mean feat for such a large ribbed dog). But with their powerful jaws the tail soon becomes traumatised, and, in extreme cases, surgical removal of part of the tail has been tried to alleviate the problem, with very mixed results. (For more information on tail chasing, see Chapter Six.)

A LOW-MAINTENANCE BREED

Of the 26 terrier breeds recognised by the Kennel Club, the Bull Terrier presents less need for grooming than most; only the Manchester Terrier has a shorter coat. As with all short-coated breeds, a Bull Terrier usually moults twice a year, but if a dog is living in an environment with a constant temperature, moulting will be virtually continual. Shed white hairs will show up on all clothing and furniture. A good

brushing with a rubber grooming pad once a week will not only remove all loose coat, but also improve the dog's circulation (and your own). Nails should be kept short from an early age if the desired tight, high-arched cat feet are to be achieved (see Chapter Five: The Best of Care).

A legacy from his pugilistic past means the Bull Terrier has no corners; with a tight-fitting skin and short coat, a Bully is an extremely slippery customer and is difficult to catch hold of – especially when wet. The wearing of a soft collar, preferably washable, around the house will prevent many an escapee. Thick collars that will mark the coat and possibly irritate the skin should not be worn all the time.

EXERCISE

Despite a 30-plus kg *avoirdupois*, a Bull Terrier does not demand excessive exercise; he is quite content to lie in front of the fire

or sleep upside down on the sofa. An adult Bull Terrier should be capable of walking briskly for over an hour without any signs of distress. Free running in a secure park or field will build up muscle and expand the lungs, but too much exercise too young will be detrimental to the pup's growing bones and may well cause damage.

A young pup may be introduced to the big wide world as soon as vaccinations are completed and he is given the all clear by the vet, but moderate exercise on a lead will suffice. I am shocked by owners who cannot wait to expose their new puppies to all the germs, diseases and worms that lurk in our parks. One owner wanted to know if it would be a good idea to take his dog out before the vet had told him it would be safe, as he wanted to take him for a run round the nearby reservoir with the local dogs. I did point out that not only would the journey to the reservoir be stressful, but the pup was building his immunity via the vaccination course so would be more susceptible to any other infection. Added to this was the fact that anywhere near water had an increased risk of Leptospirosis, so, no, I was not in favour of his suggestion. (For information on vaccinations, see Chapter Eight: Happy and Healthy.)

The growth rate of a Bull Terrier puppy is extremely fast, so care should be taken not to over walk heavily boned puppies if

WEARING A HARNESS

There seems to be a fashion developing for using a harness rather than a collar for a Bull Terrier. A word of warning here: if a young Bull Terrier is exercised in a harness and becomes used to hanging his weight on the lead and harness, the elbows will be pushed out and cause an imperfect front.

The front legs should be underneath the body, with elbows tucked in, and the line down the leg totally straight. If a Bull Terrier is constantly hanging on a harness, the elbows will stick out and the front legs will bow, giving an incorrect Bulldog front and causing problems later in life.

Exercise should be built up gradually while a youngster is still growing.

Photo: Alice van Kempen.

the desired gun-barrel front is to be achieved. Similarly, pups chasing hard and fast after a ball may well cause problems due to their muscle power, which, in extreme cases, will cause fractures. That does not mean that Bull Terrier pups should be wrapped in cotton wool – they would only eat it – but care should be taken not to do too much lead exercise with them before they are six months old.

Some Bull Terriers will take to swimming and love water – many will simply close their eyes and sink like a stone. Similarly,

retrieving is not their forte. If you throw a ball, for a Bull Terrier, even a large leather football, it is unlikely to be serviceable when you do eventually retake possession.

As with any heavily boned breed, you should be mindful of the likelihood of arthritis developing in later years. Many proprietary complete foods now include joint supplements, but these may be given as additions to an ordinary diet and are available in capsule, tablet or liquid form, all of which will be swallowed with gusto.

A CANINE VACUUM

Bull Terriers have a phenomenal appetite. Eating is likened to vacuuming: all is sucked up extremely quickly. The normal diet is frequently supplemented with socks or toys. In fact, anything left lying around gets quickly hoovered up. So if you have untidy children who refuse to put their prized possessions away, a Bull Terrier may be the answer. I have personal experience of Action Man accessories, Lego, Matchbox toys, nails, screws and even fencing staples safely negotiating a Bull

You need to be realistic in your expectations when you are training a Bull Terrier. *Photo: Alice van Kempen.*

Terrier's digestive system. However, a proprietary complete feed will contain all the essential vitamins and minerals and be less harrowing for the owner or the child with missing toys.

On a more serious note, Bull Terriers have died from ingesting stones, rubber balls, leads and sweetcorn cobs. The need for vigilance is obvious.

TRAINABILITY

As with all terriers, a Bull Terrier has a mind of his own. Some have been successfully trained to compete in obedience, but they are the exceptions. Most Bullies have far more entertaining things to do than waste their time sitting by your side while you chat; in all probability they will have chewed through their lead

and be off to make friends with other dogs before you even notice. Sitting and staying are regarded as party pieces for special occasions when wanting to impress, or when crossing a busy main road.

The perversity of the Bull Terrier knows no bounds. I frequently remark that the best method of recall for any terrier is to shout his name and run like blazes in the opposite direction. Consequently, a Bull Terrier would not be an obvious choice as either a guide dog or a sniffer dog; they have reduced the most hardened trainers to tears of frustration. Their in-built obstinacy does not sit well with the role of an assistance dog; they are quite capable of fetching the required articles but giving them

up would be a different matter, and, should they oblige, the condition of the article would probably be far from pristine. Yet their love of people and attention, combined with an audience for entertaining, enables them to act as successful therapy dogs and they will bring many a smile to the faces of those they visit.

LIVING WITH OTHER DOGS

In general, Bull Terriers are amiable and will tolerate other dogs, but consideration must be taken of the sheer size and power of a Bully. Hurtling around a park or field at full tilt, there are few breeds robust enough to withstand such impact. Tall, leggy dogs with narrow ribcages could be felled as trees, and most small breeds will be negated and left floundering in their wake. Breeds taller than Bullies and at least of similar weight would be most suited as running mates.

A Bully will live harmoniously with other breeds if introduced at an early age, and will even tolerate cats on the same basis. Bull Terrier bitches are generally very maternal and will take on young puppies or kittens and happily mother them.

Expecting a Bull Terrier to ignore a pet rabbit or hamster is asking too much. No doubt there are exceptions, but it must be remembered that, in common with all terriers, anything that moves quickly will trigger the instinct to grab first and think later. Those Bull Terrier jaws are extremely powerful and quick.

THE MINIATURE BULL TERRIER

The Miniature Bull Terrier is exactly what it says: all of the above but smaller. An ideal height of 35.5 cms (14 ins) is stated in the Breed Standard, requesting an impression of substance to the size of the dog. Though, again, no weight limit is given, it is essential that the dog should be balanced.

Back in the 1970s it was not uncommon to see tiny Miniature Bull Terriers, short on the leg and long in their back; they were well under the height required but lacked that elusive quality known as 'type'. Some were more reminiscent of Lancashire Heelers in their proportions. Despite the setback of the hereditary eye

condition lens luxation, which caused a great deal of problems and the loss of many bloodlines, the Miniature Bull Terrier of today is a more accurate replica of its standard relative than ever before.

My favourite descriptive word for a Mini is 'corky'. For me that sums up their solidity and bounciness; they are just as much fun only in a smaller package. So perhaps more suited to a small/medium suburban garden, the Mini is merely a smaller bull in a china shop racing around!

SUMMING UP

So why choose a Bull Terrier? A small, wriggling piglet will turn into a magnificent muscular dog,

attracting admiration and respect. In this metamorphosis, the chewed artefacts, craters in the garden, destroyed plants etc. will all be forgotten as your Bull Terrier stands before you, tail wagging furiously, grinning at you inanely and emanating a snuffly sort of grunt – the Bull Terrier 'love noise' that assures you that you have made the right choice.

For such an ostensibly tough dog, a Bully is remarkably affectionate, appreciative of attention, and has a well-developed sense of humour. The muscle-bound hard nut does have a soft centre – perhaps that is what gives the Bully his very special appeal.

The Miniature Bull Terrier: Just as much fun but in a smaller package.
Photo courtesy: Alan V. Walker.

THE FIRST BULL TERRIERS

Chapter 2

Bull Terriers are far from the top of the list of the most popular dogs, and so they are not among the canines we see being walked around our neighbourhoods every day. When we do see one, however, we cannot but be impressed by that initially diabolical appearance: the muscular build, the jaunty gait and that strange looking head. When the Bull Terrier suddenly and irrepressibly puts on a clownish act, we begin to question who is taking whom for a walk. Not the dog for us? Well, certainly the Bully is not for everyone. Yet those of us who own a Bully would argue that they are the most engaging and loving of companions, and they are great with kids. With a Bully as part of the family, there is rarely a dull moment.

To begin to understand the Bully, we need to go back more

than 200 years. Like most of the terriers, the Bully traces his origins to the British Isles with the crossing of Bulldogs and various terriers. One such early cross, Camp, was described by Sir Walter Scott as, "*The wisest dog I have ever owned…*" Let us learn about the Bully by reviewing his development from those early days.

BULLDOG ANCESTRY

For centuries the sport of bull baiting had been enjoyed almost as a national pastime. The old-style Bulldog was used by butchers for restraining large animals, like bulls, using the simple expedient of pinning the bull by its nose. The sporting version of this activity pitched Bulldogs against tethered bulls. By the late 1700s, however, bull baiting was losing popularity to the sports of cock and dog fighting. The old-style Bulldog

was higher on the leg, longer in head, and generally more mobile than today's 'sour mug'. However, despite this mobility, plus strength, determination and proverbial courage, these Bulldogs provided but a poor spectacle in the fighting pit, lacking the speed and agility needed to excite the crowds.

Enter the lowly terriers, their name deriving from 'terra' meaning 'earth'. Bred to go to ground and to kill vermin, terriers were – and, to a large degree, still are – high spirited, aggressive, agile and quick to respond. They complemented the Bulldog in every essential respect and soon Bulldog-terrier crosses became the choice of the dog fighting fraternity. Some preferred three-quarters Bulldog and one-quarter terrier, others a straight cross.

These crosses varied considerably in shape, colour and size. But these physical

The old type of Bulldog was bred to bait bulls. This type was higher in the leg, and longer in the head than the Bulldog we know today.

characteristics were unimportant; what mattered was their performance in the dog pit. Small dogs began to be pitted against rats, their challenge being to kill a specified number of rats in the shortest time. They were known by various names: Bulldog-terrier, Bull-and-terriers and eventually as Bull-terriers. In 1833-43, Sir William Jardine (editor of the collection referred to as the Naturalist Library) commented that, *"the breed called Bull-terriers… constitutes the most determined and savage race known."* Their success, however, heralded the demise of the old Bulldogs; they had lost their job as surely as plough horses lost out to tractors a century later.

CHANGING TIMES

The Humane Act of 1835 finally outlawed bull baiting. The Act also banned dog fighting, though it appeared to have little impact on the sport at the time. These activities simply went underground. But other social changes were emerging. Hitherto dogs, other than a relatively few 'pets' owned by the aristocracy, had had to earn their food and keep; some were guard dogs, others herded sheep or hunted fox and deer. The general public owned dogs that helped them with their livelihoods, as had long been the case with butchers needing Bulldogs to control fractious cattle. But in England the Victorian era fostered the emergence of a new and wealthy middle class, whose members could afford to own dogs for no useful purpose other than to demonstrate their social status. Such dogs were to become known as pet and prize animals.

By the 1850s some public houses were advertising ratting events – possibly accompanied by now illegal dog fights – and also what were referred to as 'leads'. These were, in essence, informal dog shows, at which the canines competed against each other not on the basis of performance but rather what we now call conformation. The first formal dog show was staged near Newcastle in 1859, soon followed by a larger show in the city of Birmingham. These new events gained rapidly in popularity.

THE WHITE CAVALIERS

An exhibitor at the early shows staged in Birmingham was a local man, one James Hinks, a poulterer and later a publican by trade. Hinks was also a respected dog dealer, especially well known for his Bulldogs, the best of which was a white dog called Madman. After early successes with Madman, Hinks turned his attention to breeding and showing Bull Terriers, for which classes were also scheduled. It should be noted that the Bull Terriers shown at these first shows were a motley crew, varying in colour and type. Hinks set about breeding a new, more refined Bull Terrier, longer and cleaner in the muzzle and distinguished by a pure white coat. He also bred White English Terriers, now extinct but much like a Manchester Terrier in conformation, and we know that he used these terriers to both refine his new dogs and to obtain the white coats.

His first winner, Puss, was born in August 1861 and took first prize at the Cremorne show in London in 1863. Reputedly she fought and killed a bigger, coloured Bull Terrier bitch before being shown, thus establishing the gameness of Hinks' new-style dogs. But we now view this tale as apocryphal. Next, Hinks mated Puss to his old Bulldog Madman. This mating produced the first great show Bull Terrier, also named Madman, who was born in December 1862. As an aside, in these early days, names like Madman, Rebel, Nelson and Puss were given to many Bull Terriers. Indeed, Hinks bred a series of males he named Madman. He took both Madman and his dam, Puss, to the 1864 Cremorne show, with Madman taking first prize and his dam going second.

For several years Hinks' dogs dominated the show scene, so it is surprising that by 1869 he had sold most of his kennel and retired from showing. By this time, however, his style of Bull Terrier was well established and often referred to as White Cavaliers due to the hallmark white coats. The old-fashioned dogs, mostly coloured and much coarser in build, were still around, but they were ousted from the show ring. Eventually they became known as Staffordshire Bull Terriers, which today, of course, is a distinct and highly popular breed.

James Hinks is the undisputed founder of the modern Bull Terrier. We know that he employed existing Bull Terriers, English White Terriers, Bulldogs

The Dalmatian was just one of the breeds used to create the Bull Terrier.

and Dalmatians in developing his White Cavaliers. It is suspected that he may have added Spanish Pointer and even Greyhound to the mix. The Hinks legacy was carried forward to the turn of the century by his son, Fred, and then, after World War One, by his eldest son, James Junior, and grandson, Carleton, who formed the highly successful Brum kennels. For many years after Hinks' death, in 1878, Birmingham remained the focal point of the breed. Later the Californian S.N. Jewot captured the essence of Hinks' contribution in his poem:

Hinks of Birmingham,
Hinks of Brum,
Found a Bull Terrier,
A tattered old bum,
Made him a right 'un,
Made him a white 'un,
Made him a dog for a
gentleman's chum.

The mantle of Madman was taken on by top prize winners (Old) Victor and his son, Young Victor, both of whom were cleaner and more refined in head than Hinks' dogs. Old Victor, a dog of unknown pedigree from the Black Country, began his show career in 1868. Mated to an all-white bitch, he sired Young Victor, who sported a coloured patch on his head at a time when any marks were frowned upon. His successes in the show ring were controversial to say the least and he was referred to as the patched or mark-eyed dog. Sadly, both died relatively young, the sire being smothered in his kennel and the son poisoned at a dog show in 1875.

EARLY CHAMPIONS
During these early days there was no controlling body in the sport. Then, in 1873, a group of prominent breeders and exhibitors formed the Kennel Club (KC). The Kennel Club's first stud book was published late in 1874 and so, prior to this date, we have to depend on show catalogues for pedigrees, ownership and the like. The first chairman of the Kennel Club was Sewallis Shirley, an MP from Warwickshire and an exhibitor of

Bull Terriers. It was Shirley's Nelson, a dog bred in Birmingham, who in 1873 became the breed's first Champion. Interestingly, Nelson weighed in at about 16 lb (7.25 kg) and so, by today's standards, would be a Miniature. In those days, Bull Terriers could be small or large, with classes divided by weight – above and below 16 lb (7.25 kg), sometimes 18 lb (8.15 kg). Shirley's support of Bull Terriers did much to enhance their reputation and status at a time when leading canine journalist Stonehenge still viewed them as crosses and others still associated them with the fighting pits.

In 1876 Tarquin became the first full-sized Bull Terrier Champion. A son of Young Victor, he weighed about 45 lb (20.5 kg) and, like his sire, was reputedly an ill-tempered dog. We have to wait until the 1880s for further Champions. An important sire at this time was Fred Hinks' (Old) Dutch, while J. Platt's Ch. Maggie May, who gained her title in 1884, became one of the great dams in breed history. She produced no fewer than five Champions before being exported to America, where she continued to excel in the whelping box. Ch. Gully the Great, a grandson of Maggie May, was made up in 1889 and went on to become a leading sire.

The 1880s and 1890s saw several breeders, whose contributions spanned many

Tarquin: The first full-sized Champion, made up in 1876.

decades, join the Bull Terrier ranks. Fred North made up Ch. Streatham Monarch, who sired Ch. Streatham Monarch II and his litter sister, Ch. Hanover Daisy. Woodcote Wonder, owned by W. Pegg, became a Champion in 1896, the first of many for his owner. We also saw the arrival on the scene of Harry Monk (Bloomsbury), W. Ely (Hampstead), Billie Tuck and that great character Tom Gannaway. We should note that Charles Cruft, who organised his first show in 1886, was a staunch supporter of the breed.

Since Hinks' pioneering efforts the breed has been gaining both in strength and popularity. The Bull Terrier Club was established in 1887. The road ahead appeared rosy. But in 1895 the Kennel Club imposed a ban on ear cropping; dogs born after that date could not be shown with cropped ears. This was followed in 1899 with a parliamentary ban

on cropping. The impact on the breed was simply devastating. For years Bull Terriers had been bred with the large thick ears that were best suited to cropping; with ugly uncropped ears these dogs lost much of their appeal. Registrations dropped dramatically and a number of supporters switched to other breeds. The impact was such that by the early 1900s, it was generally accepted that the breed was much stronger in America, where cropping was acceptable until the 1950s. Many of the top winners had also made the trip across the Atlantic.

WHITE CAVALIERS IN AMERICA

Bulldog-terrier crosses were exported to America from their earliest days and there was a resurgence of importations of the old-style Bull Terriers after the Civil War. Dog fighting was a popular pastime in cities such as New York and Boston, and flourished long after the sport, so called, had effectively disappeared in the UK. Over time they became known as America Pit Bull Terriers; some continued as fighting dogs but others took on the role of working dogs for the homesteaders, who settled across the American west. In the process they became bigger and taller than the English Staffordshire Bull Terriers. During the 1930s a group of Pit Bulls were taken into the pet and prize arena, becoming American Staffordshire Terriers or Am Staffs for short.

Meanwhile Hinks' new style of dogs gained a rapid and strong foothold in the United States. Strangely enough, the first Bull Terrier registered by the American Kennel Club (AKC) was the brindle bitch Nellie II (in 1885). The earliest recorded benched show took place in Chicago in 1876, with the first Westminster Kennel Club show taking place the following year. Of the 11 Bull Terriers entered at Westminster, two were brindles, the others whites. The leading breeder and exhibitor in America was Frank Dole, who began importing Bull Terrier from England in 1884. Among his imports were the famous Ch. Maggie May, who produced from him the wonderful bitch Ch. Starlight, and Champions Gully the Great and Woodcote Wonder. Fred Hinks exported numerous dogs, including a number sired by Old Dutch.

The American Kennel Club began recording Champions in its *Kennel Gazette* in 1889. There were seven that first year, all English imports. Starlight became the first American-bred Champion, albeit from two

A seaman pictured with his Bull Terrier around 1914.

imports, in 1890. All told, 30 Bull Terriers gained their American Championships prior to 1900.

Following those first shows, there was no mention of coloured Bull Terriers. The Bull Terrier Club of America (BTCA) was founded in 1897 after an abortive earlier attempt. Fanciers in America took to their White Cavaliers with a passion. Indeed, it was they who later resisted the introduction of the coloured Bull Terrier to the bitter end.

THE BREED EVOLVES

The Bull Terrier as we know him today owes much to the changes

and developments made by breeders in the UK in the first half of the 20th century. Their first challenge was to produce a neater ear, the goal being a smaller, thinner, prick type. This proved to be a surprisingly irksome task. Although it was accomplished in large part by the 1920s, to this day some Bull Terrier puppies need help with getting their ears up.

Another development concerned the shape of the head. The absence of a stop had long been a distinctive feature, but, just after the turn of the century, fanciers began to talk about a 'down-ness' or 'down-face', meaning that rather than the skull and muzzle being flat, there should be an arc or curvature to the head when viewed in profile. By 1915 the new English Standard called for an egg-shaped head with the profile curving from occiput to nose, the more 'down-faced' the better. This unique head shape became the Holy Grail for breeders. Now that we have both white and coloured Bull Terriers, the egg-shaped head is the hallmark of the breed rather than Hinks' pure white coat. Developing the modern head with that spectacular down-face took focus and many generations to achieve. We saw significant progress in the 1920s and again after World War Two. The 1970s gave us heads that met the description in the Breed Standards by any and every rational measure. But this was – and is – not enough for breeders focussed on top prizes, and so for the past 20 years, we have been attempting and succeeding in exaggerating the egg.

The third major development concerned coat colour. On his return from India, where he had hunted with old-style coloured Bull Terriers, Ted Lyon (Sher) viewed the White Cavaliers as too soft, lacking the spirit and gameness he demanded. In response he decided to backcross White Cavaliers with Staffordshires to regain that gameness. In this quest, which began in 1907, he was aided and abetted by Harry Tumner. Their task was formidable, primarily because of the differences in head and expression: a Staffordshire having a short, wide head with a distinct stop and round, open eyes. It was not until 1919 that the brindle Bing Boy became the first coloured Bull Terrier to win a Challenge Certificate, and we had

Ch. Romany Rhinestone: A coloured Bull Terrier of outstanding quality. *Photo: Fall.*

to wait until 1931 for the first coloured Champion when Lady Winfred was made up. It was in 1937 that Miss Montague Johnstone's Ch. Romany Rhinestone would finally match the whites in both head and expression, but it would be many more decades before the coloureds attained equality in terms of both overall type and popularity.

The key dog at the turn of the century was Gannaway's Ch. Charlwood Victor Wild, who is behind every Bull Terrier today. The dominant breeder and exhibitor up until World War One was undoubtedly Harry Monk, to whom, Raymond Oppenheimer wrote, "*must go the credit for assembling the breed for the first time into a coherent whole.*" Monk was also a great showman,

whose Bloomsbury Champions came off the production line in regular succession; Ch. Bloomsbury Cheeky was virtually unbeatable in his day.

In 1911, North's White Noel became the first Champion with fully prick ears, it is believed. His son, Ch. Krishna, was an outstanding show dog. Ely kept his Hampstead dogs to the fore, while Gannaway's Hampstead Heathen and Monk's Bloomsbury Czar both excelled at stud. Tuck doubled up on Czar to produce the famous Lord Gladiator, a super headed, if rather unsound, specimen, who is credited as the font of the modern head. Mention must also be made of the beloved Mrs Adlam (Granny Adie), who began her 60 years in the breed circa 1909.

POST-WAR PROGRESS
Carleton Hinks and his father came to the fore in the 1920s. They purchased Ely's Ch. Hades Cavalier, who sired for them the outstanding Champion brothers White Wonder and Wonder's Double. Unfortunately, both were exported. Meanwhile Lord

Gladiator began to exert an enormous influence on the breed, improving heads – though often having a negative impact on conformation. Several of Lord Gladiator's sons and grandsons were terrific sires, dominating the top (male) of nearly all pedigrees.

The most successful was his grandson, Ch. Crookes Great Boy, who is behind every leading Bull Terrier of later generations. Great Boy's daughter, Ch. White Rose Girl, was unquestionably the best bitch to that date and for many years to come; in the show ring, she was unbeatable. While Lord Gladiator dominated the top line, most of the other lines can be traced back to Ely's Hampstead dogs and Gannaway's Lillingtons (the affix he now used). The framework for the tremendous advances of the 1930s had been established.

The year 1929 saw Mrs Adlam's famous and much-loved Ch. Rhoma complete her Championship. Her sire was reputedly deaf – a significant problem in those days. In 1930, Dr Geoffrey Vevers (Regent) donated the Regent Trophy to the Bull Terrier Club, to be awarded annually to the best Bull Terrier first shown the previous year; the first award went to a daughter of Rhoma. The 1931 Regent Trophy

THE END OF THE SMALL TERRIER

The Great War marked the demise of small Bull Terriers. A cadre of wealthy breeders brought them down in size to less than 12 lb (5.45 kg) with some as small as just 3 lbs (1.36 kg) – essentially Toy dogs. By 1922 they were no longer being shown and were struck off the list of registered breeds by the Kennel Club. Efforts to bring back a bigger type began in the late 1930 and, of course, today we have the Miniature Bull Terriers as a distinct breed.

went to Ch. Ringfire of Blighty, essentially Birmingham bloodlines, but inevitably with the top line going back to Lord Gladiator. It was his brother, Rubislaw, however, who became a dominant sire, producing a number of great bitches, including the 1933 trophy winner.

Unquestionably, the top breeder of the mid-1930s was Harry Potter, whose Gardenia dogs won four Regent Trophies. Potter was a brilliant exponent of the half-brother half-sister breeding, followed by an outcross. His first two Champions, Gardenia and his full brother Gardenia Guardsman, were doubled up on Vever's Regent Pluto (a great grandson of Crookes Great Boy).

Inevitably the breeding of coloured Bull Terriers resulted in number of white as well as coloured puppies. These whites were considered the equivalent of mongrels and breeders were expected to 'bucket' them and certainly not to show them or use them to produce white offspring. However, in 1936 Rebel of Blighty, the white son of two brindles, was shown and became a Champion. The establishment was outraged by this first 'colour-bred white' Champion. To guarantee all white parentage, the Bull Terrier Club set up the 'white stud book'.

Meanwhile, a number of coloured Champions were crowned, the most important of which were Jane of Petworth and Miss Montague Johnstone's Romany Rhinestone, the first coloured to match the whites in head. To Miss Johnstone, one of the truly great breeders, must go the kudos for raising the type and quality of the colours on to an equal footing.

ILLUSTRIOUS BLOODLINES
The sensation of the brindle post-war period was the great-headed brindle Ch. Romany Reliance, bred by Miss Johnstone with lines back to Brigadier, Vindicator, McGuffin and Rhinestone. Like most of the coloureds, Reliance had a lot of the top whites close

FOUNDATION SIRES

Ch. Ormandy's Mr McGuffin: Famed for his substance and his tiny, black eyes.
Photo: Fall.

Ch. Raydium Brigadier: A Bull Terrier of great style.

Ch. Velhurst Vindicator: A heavyweight dog with a classical head.

Ch. Abraxas Audacity: Crufts Best in Show, 1972.
Photo: Fall.

THE MODERN BULL TERRIER

The Regent Trophy winners for 1937-1939, Champions Raydium Brigadier, Velhurst Vindicator and Ormandy's Mr. McGuffin, laid the foundation for the modern Bull Terrier. Brigadier was doubled up on Guardsman; that is by a son of Guardsman out of one of his daughters. Owned by Mrs Adlam, he excelled in profile and personified style.

Next came Mrs Phillips' Vindicator, sired by a grandson of her Velhurst Viking (a son of Pluto) out of one of his granddaughters. Vindicator, built along classical lines, offered wonderful type and quality.

Finally, there was McGuffin, the first of Raymond Oppenheimer's many Champions. To date none of the great Rubislaw daughters had produced anything worthwhile, so newcomer Oppenheimer – against expert advice – decided to double up on ill-tempered Rubislaw. His hunch proved correct when the mating produced McGuffin, with his wonderful bone and substance and tiny black eyes.

These three dogs, together with Rhinestone for the coloureds, combined to advance the breed and are behind all of today's Bull Terriers.

up in his pedigree. Miss Johnstone was joined by Miss Meg Williams and together they bred many more illustrious Romanys. Meanwhile, Oppenheimer bred Ch. Ormandy's Dancing Time (sired by Vindicator out of a McGuffin daughter), who was considered to be the best Bull Terrier all around and years ahead of her time. Oppenheimer was joined at Ormandy by Miss Eva Weatherill (Souperlative) and together they formed a formidable team. The Ormandy-Souperlative dogs gained worldwide fame and Oppenheimer assumed the role of patron and leader of 'Bull Terrierdom' worldwide.

The fancy eventually recognised that white Bull Terriers are, in fact, coloureds with a genetic factor inhibiting the expression of colour, and so all are colour-bred. The white stud book was discontinued, and the so-called colour-bred whites began to exert a significant influence on the breed. Two key colour-bred sires were Ch. The Sphinx and his son, Ch. Beechhouse Snow Vision (out of a Reliance daughter). Supremely shapely, The Sphinx again combined Brigadier, Vindicator and McGuffin with coloured lines. Snow Vision, who gained his title in 1953, became one of the greatest sires and contributed much to the advancement of the breed.

A year later we saw the appearance of the last of the great 'pure white' dogs – Ch. Souperlative Snowflash, bred by Miss Weatherill and owned by Oppenheimer. His pedigree features Brigadier and other Raydium dogs in the top half, with the usual Vindicator/McGuffin combination in the bottom half. Snowflash went on to sire what was a record number of Champions – among them Miss Graham Weall's beautiful Ch. Phidgity Snow Dream – but, interestingly, all came from coloured or colour-bred bitches.

Snow Vision, mated to Snowflash's litter sister, produced Miss Weatherill's Ch. Souperlative Summer Queen, the dam of a record seven English Champions; while to Snow Dream he sired the key stud dog, Ch. Phidgity Phlasher of Lenster. Then Romany mated a son of The

Typical coloured Bull Terriers from the Romany bloodlines. In the US, the coloured variety caused huge controversy.

Sphinx to a daughter of Snow Vision. The result was the brindle Ch. Romany Robin Goodfellow, certainly the greatest coloured of that time and the first Bull Terrier to win Best in Show at an all breed Championship show in England. Type and quality were moving ahead in leaps and bounds.

The 1960s saw it all come together, as the leading breeders combined the virtues of Snow Vision and Snowflash. At Ormandy, Miss Weatherill doubled up on Snow Vision by mating Summer Queen to Phlasher. From this litter came three celebrated Champions: Ormandy Souperlative Chunky, Ormandy Souperlative Princeling, and Souperlative Brinhead. Miss Weall sent Snow Dream to Robin Goodfellow, which produced the outstanding white Ch. Romany

Romantic Vision, the sire of many wonderful bitches. To a bitch line-bred to Snowflash, Princeling sired Ch. Ormandy's Ben of Highthorpe, who later sired Miss Weatherill's beautiful Ch. Souperlative Rominten Rheingold.

Then, in late 1962, came a flashpoint at Ormandy, with a litter sired by Brinhead out of Ch. Souperlative Sunshine, a daughter of Romantic Vision and Summer Queen, thus doubling up on Summer Queen. From this tight line-breeding came Champions Souperlative Sea Captain Sea and Masta Plasta of Ormandy. And, most importantly, Ormandy Souperlative Bar Sinister, so called because he had only one descended testicle. This apart, Bar Sinister was said to be "*appreciably in advance of any previous Bull Terrier*". After deliberation Oppenheimer decided to offer Bar

Sinister at stud, in which capacity he excelled, siring a number of superb dogs and bitches, including, out of a daughter of Ben, the key sire Ch. Monkery's Mr Frosty of Ormandy.

At Romany, Misses Johnstone and Williams mated lovely coloured daughters of Romantic Vision and Robin Goodfellow to Sea Captain and Brinhead respectively. From this came the great brindle sire Ch. Romany River Pirate. Miss Violet Drummond-Dick (Abraxas) came to the fore when she mated a granddaughter of Romantic Vision and Summer Queen to Mr Frosty and got the beautiful Ch. Abraxas Athenia, dam of three successive Regent Trophy winners. From Athenia's first litter came Ch. Abraxas Audacity, who, like his sire River Pirate, was a terrific showman. In 1972 Audacity became the first and only Bull Terrier to become Supreme Champion at Crufts. As show dogs, Bull Terriers were reaching new heights, from which they have not looked back. The modern era had arrived.

These same lines continued to be combined, leading to great-headed Ch. Souperlative Jackadandy of Ormandy – born in 1976 – breaking all breed records as the sire of 21 English Champions. Since then, the primary quest has been for ever more dramatically down-faced heads, even at the expense of width and depth of muzzle. In parallel the coloureds are no longer the underdogs, having moved on to an essentially equal

INFLUENTIAL BLOODLINES

Am. Can. Ch. Monkery's Buckskin: Leading American sire 1980-1984, producing a record number of Champions.

Am. Ch. Banbury Benson of Bedrock: Leading sire of the early 1980s, and the first coloured Bully to win the Terrier Group at Westminster in 1982.

footing with the whites in the show ring.

THE BULL TERRIER IN AMERICA

In the early 1900s the White Cavaliers, still with cropped ears, thrived in America. The top winners were Frank Dole's Ch. Woodcote Wonder and the Gartner brothers' Ch. Princeton Monarch, American-bred but sired by a British import. In 1904 the Westminster Kennel Club show provided a magnificent entry of 147 for English judge W. Pegg, who was impressed by both their soundness and movement. The Canadian-bred dog Haymarket Faultless, later a Champion, demonstrated these same virtues when he took Best in Show at Westminster in 1918 – the equivalent of winning Crufts. This, however, proved to be the high point for Bull Terriers in America.

During the 1920s breeders lamented the superior dogs of 20 years ago. Despite the new 1915 Breed Standard, which closely paralleled the English version, the preferred type in America remained a Bully that was higher on the leg, sounder in conformation and without the down-face and egg-shaped head that was by then the rage across the Atlantic. There were even arguments that the head should be brick-shaped, without any curvature. Imports continued to arrive, but these new-style dogs were unpopular among the traditionalists. So, while British breeders took up the gauntlet of developing the modern head, often at the expense of soundness, the breed in America fell into the doldrums.

In 1933 the imported Rubislaw daughter Ch. Faultless of Blighty took Best in Show at the prestigious Montgomery County

show for terriers. The leading breeder of the decade was Mrs Jessie Platt Bennett with her Coolyn Hill dogs, which were founded on several top-class imports. From these imports came Ch. Coolyn Bailfire, a leading stud, and his lovely daughter, Ch. Coolyn Quicksilver, who excelled in the show ring.

But it was the coloureds that hit the headlines. In 1934 the first two coloured Bull Terriers arrived from England. To the members of the Bull Terrier Club of America (BTCA), this was like waving a red flag in front of a bull. They were outraged that these mongrels might taint their pure white lines and wanted them treated as a separate breed. Even worse, in 1937 the colour-bred white Rebel of Blighty arrived in America. The breed club fought to keep their White Cavaliers completely separate. However, the American Kennel

Am. Ch. Rocky's Top Thunder Storm: 2004 Silverwood Trophy winner.

Club held the upper hand and the best the BTCA could achieve was for whites and coloureds to be divided as separate varieties of the same breed. And so it has remained to this day. At shows they compete in separate classes for best of variety, meeting only in the Terrier Group or for Best of Breed at independent Specialty shows. This means that even coloured and white siblings do not compete against each other in the classes.

Given the restrictions of World War Two, Mrs Adlam decided to send Raydium Brigadier to America, where he was purchased by Mrs Bennett. His arrival finally turned the tide in favour of the new-style English dogs. At stud Brigadier exerted enormous impact on the breed. His best son, out of an imported bitch,

was Doctor Montgomery's Ch. Heir Apparent to Monty-Ayr. Colourful and quite literally larger than life, Doc Montgomery (Monty-Ayr) became the leading figure on the American scene, importing and breeding many, many Bull Terriers through the 1950s. But despite regular infusions of British stock, American Bull Terriers failed to match their counterparts across the Atlantic in type and quality. A top-winning import would arrive and produce outstanding progeny, but within a couple of generations the gains would be lost and breeders would look to the next import.

SILVERWOOD TROPHY WINNERS

This state of affairs persisted until the late 1960s when efforts began

to emulate the English trophy competition. The first Silverwood Trophy event was staged in 1970, bringing into competition the best North American-bred Bull Terriers and attracting breeders and fanciers from across this geographically dispersed community. Since then, the Silverwood weekend has been held annually and is credited with providing the spark that has led to the continued and sustained improvement of the breed in America. The late 1960s also saw the appearance of two kennels – Banbury (Mrs Winkie Mackay-Smith) and, in Canada, Magor (Norma and Gordon Smith) – that have contributed enormously to this improvement. Over the decades both kennels have bred top-class stock, including numerous Silverwood winners, and offered many outstanding males at stud.

Mrs Mackay-Smith dominated the second Silverwood competition with the littermates Champions Banbury Charity Buttercup and Banbury Briar and in 1976 the Smiths won their first Silverwood with Ch. Magor the Marquis. These three winners each resulted from mating an imported Regent Trophy-winning male to a beautifully bred imported bitch. However, both kennels were able to sustain type and quality without constant resort to imports and this has shown the way to other breeders, ensuring that the best Bull Terriers in North America can match those in the UK and around the world.

The modern Bull Terrier: Ch. Bullbrit Little Big Horn at Bullyview won 18 CCs and broke the breed record for CCs after 97 years.

MODERN TIMES

Bull Terriers continue to flourish in both Britain and America. For many years registrations in both countries hovered in the 1,000-1,200 range, and, until the past five years, had remained so in America. In Britain, however, numbers have climbed significantly since around 1980. In part this increase reflects the higher demand for puppies at home and for export. It also reflects the profit motive. Around 40 to 50 years ago, for most fanciers their involvement in breeding and exhibiting Bull Terriers was barely if at all profitable; since then, selling puppies and winning adults has become a significant source of additional income. In turn, more puppies place increasing pressure on rescue and welfare organisations. This calls for responsible breeders and responsible breeding.

With these numbers, Bull Terriers are not at the top of the canine popularity stakes. They are in the middle of the pack, which has its advantages. Popularity leads to back-street breeding, while at the other end of the spectrum low number breeds have such small gene pools.

Whatever the challenges, Bull Terriers continue to offer their families unfailing devotion and companionship. Yes, they can be overly enthusiastic, mischievous and demanding of attention. But this is balanced by their comic nature and their love of people.

NUMBER OF BULL TERRIERS REGISTERED		
YEAR	KENNEL CLUB	AKC
1998	2523	941
1999	2632	1004
2000	2925	1093
2001	2419	1072
2002	2665	1190
2003	2924	1357
2004	2996	1548
2005	3210	1744
2006	3361	1765
2007	3335	1821

A BULL TERRIER FOR YOUR LIFESTYLE

Chapter 3

So you have decided that you want a Bull Terrier to be your companion for the next 12 years. Whose choice was this? Does everyone in the household agree or are they just trying to humour you, hoping it is a passing phase and that you will change your mind as soon as you spot another unusual dog?

A family conference might be worthwhile in the long run! After all, some family members might not know anything about the breed you want to take on. A trip to the library for a book containing photographs is a useful first step, and you can also find out about the breed on the internet.

There are many factors to consider when choosing a breed to suit your lifestyle:

- **Short- or long-haired?** Who does the vacuuming?
- **Short- or long-legged?** Who does the exercising?
- **Size of appetite:** Who is paying for the food, biscuits, kibble and bones?
- **Additional expenses:** Can you afford routine health care, such as annual booster inoculations, not to mention veterinary treatment from time to time?
- **Insurance:** You may well find that the pup has been insured for a short term to cover his journey to his new home and the settling-in period. Once this has expired, you should insure the pup for yourself to protect you against veterinary fees and any damage or accidents that your dog may cause.
- **Holidays:** If you cannot take your dog on holiday with you, you will need to find boarding kennels.
- **Training:** All dogs need socialising and training. This takes time and patience. Who is prepared to take on this task?
- **Responsibility:** After everyone has left the house for their daily activity, it is usually Mum who is left with this bundle of fun. Does she really want this?
- **Work commitments:** A dog should not be left alone for more than four hours a day. If you work longer hours, you will need to consider employing a dog sitter or a dog walker to care for your dog in your absence.

WHY CHOOSE A BULL TERRIER?

Once you come to know a Bull Terrier, you will never want another breed. If you fall victim to his charm, no other dog will have the same hold over you. A Bull Terrier should be good-natured, friendly, patient, outgoing, adaptable and

The Bull Terrier is well known for his love of children.

completely loyal. The Bully is extremely affectionate to his own family and is renowned for his love of children. He is mischievous, playful, and loves to act the clown.

The Bull Terrier needs to be taught about every situation, which is a time-consuming but worthwhile occupation. A Bully needs to listen to a strange noise or look at something unfamiliar and decide that there is nothing to worry about. He will soon lose interest and take the situation in his stride, but it is a breed trait that all members of the family should be aware of.

Bull Terriers have a happy knack of considering that all children, particularly babies, should be cared for. As a nine-month-old child, my husband

crawled into the hearth of an unguarded, coal-burning fire, whereupon the family Bull Terrier grabbed him by the back of his clothing and carried him to safety. His paws were severely burnt.

A Bully will not dream of harming a child, but supervision is needed at all times, as children get excited and play rough games. Inevitably the dog joins in with the rough-and-tumble, and neither children nor dog know when to stop. It is important to remember that the pup needs rest and it is wise to teach the children in the household to respect this and ensure that the pup is put to rest in his crate at regular intervals.

While you are at this decision-making stage, it is worth agreeing

on whether to have a puppy or an older animal. Puppies are hard work, but an adult may be difficult or stubborn if he is set in his ways.

STANDARD OR MINIATURE?

There are two varieties of Bull Terrier: the popular standard size, and the miniature, which is rarely seen. The Kennel Club of Great Britain allowed inter-breeding between standards and miniatures until January 1988, which improved the type and substance of the minis.

The miniatures should be no more than 10 to 14 inches (25-35 cm) at the withers and most weigh between 15 and 30 pounds (6.8 to 13.6 kg). Although varying greatly in

Miniature Bull Terriers are quite rare and you will need to find a specialist breeder. *Photo courtesy: Alan V. Walker.*

temperament – some are easygoing, others energetic bundles – they are sturdy dogs, living to 10-12 years. They are comfort loving, clownish, mischievous, stubborn and curious. They require special and responsible owners, tolerant of destructive pups that need to be closely supervised. While being marvellous mothers and very affectionate to their owners, they are feisty animals and need to be handled firmly compared to the more laidback standard Bull Terriers.

If you would like a mini, you will need to meet the breeders, for they are very choosy about who they will sell a puppy to. There are not many minis born each year and if there is a slump in bitch puppies, it will mean fewer breeding bitches in generations to come. Health problems in Miniatures are the same as those in full-sized Bull Terriers, with one addition – lens luxation. This eye problem is a serious inherited disease that leads to blindness.

The Bull Terrier and the Miniature Bull Terrier are both extremely expensive; the price reflects the quality of care and rearing that has gone into their breeding.

EXERCISE

Exercise requirements will vary from dog to dog. Some Bull Terriers enjoy unlimited walking while others will satisfy their needs within the confines of the house and garden. Generally, a Bully will fit in with his owner's habits. Human companionship is what he really wants. A Bull Terrier does not mind what the family is doing so long as he can be part of the action, too. Bear in mind that a Bull Terrier is not a guard dog and will not take kindly to being left outside to take care of the premises.

MALE OR FEMALE?

Choosing a male or female (dog or bitch) is a matter of personal preference. Both sexes are equally loyal yet independent. If there is an exciting adventure ahead, the male will be off but the female will just check up on the family first – they may be doing something even better. Bull Terriers don't mind what they do, provided they are doing it with you!

If you want a bitch, there are some breeders who will only sell their stock on breeding terms.

If you take on a bitch, you will have to cope with her seasonal cycle unless you have her neutered.

Unless you plan to breed with a male, neutering may be a better option.

You need to think carefully about this. It means that you make an arrangement in which the bitch is sold to you at a slightly lower price, but you agree to breed with her, and the bitch's breeder will have pick of the litter when the puppies are born. However, it usually means that the breeder is willing to help with problems of whelping and the future of the pups. So it is up to you.

If you do not neuter your Bull Terrier, there are additional problems to deal with. One of our stud dogs would roam for five miles to reach a farm on the moors in the hope of seeing his lady love. The police would collect him and bring him home sitting on the back seat of their car! A bitch can also be very

determined and will try to escape from your premises when she is in season, so you will need to be on security alert.

A bitch can be very erratic up to three weeks before she comes into season. You often do not recognise the signs unless you have checked the dates in the diary. There are several anti-mate sprays available that can be used during these three weeks, and all but the most persistent dogs will take the hint and leave her alone.

Males can be neutered after six months of age. If a dog is boisterous and unruly, neutering is often an effective solution. In most cases, a Bully will gradually calm down and become more concerned with the family activities. A bitch can be spayed

after her first or second season; the best plan is to seek veterinary advice.

MORE THAN ONE?

By selective breeding, most of the old fighting tendencies have been bred out, but the Bull Terrier should not be completely trusted with other animals. Disputes between dogs over ownership of gloves, toys or even an insect can rapidly become far more serious when a Bull Terrier is involved. It is wise to have facilities available to keep two dogs separated when the owners are out, particularly if they are both males. Two bitches may live in greater harmony, but one of each sex is even less wearing.

Bull Terriers do get along together, but beware of disputes over toys and other items of value, as these can quickly escalate. *Photo: Alice van Kempen.*

LIVING WITH OTHER ANIMALS

The Bull Terrier is a tolerant dog and will learn to live in harmony with other animals. However, introductions must be carefully supervised, and all interactions should be monitored until your Bully understands how he should behave. In time, a sense of mutual respect will be established, and Bull Terriers have made good companions with cats, rabbits and even some horses.

COLOURS AND MARKINGS

The white Bull Terrier should have a pure white coat, though markings above the collar, such as a coloured ear or an eye patch, are acceptable. It is interesting to note that white Bull Terriers are not albinos; the white is a colour that has been subjected to an inhibiting factor.

Some markings enhance a dog's appearance while others have an adverse effect. For example, a white head with black patches surrounding the eyes may look very cute when a puppy is in the nest, but when he turns to look at you in the show ring, it is rather like a pair of car headlights approaching!

The coloured Bull Terriers can be seen in brindle, black brindle, red fawn and tri-colour, brindle being the dominant colour. Usually the coloured Bull Terriers have a white blaze on the head, a white chest, white under the belly, four white socks and a white tip to their tail. A coloured Bully should have more colour than white visible – the colour should predominate. If you are buying a puppy for show, it is worth noting that a coloured marking tucking well round the tummy helps to make the dog look well made.

Markings below the neck on a white Bull Terrier are called mismarks; they are not encouraged in the show dog, but are perfectly acceptable for pet dogs. These dogs often have flecks of colour in their coat, which are known as ticks. In this instance, the breeder may offer you a slightly reduced price, as the dog has a fault that makes him unsuitable for the show ring.

BULL TERRIER MARKINGS

Markings on a white dog can enhance their appearance.
Photo: Alice van Kempen.

The typical white markings on a coloured Bull Terrier.

Photo: Alice van Kempen.

HEARING TEST

If you are planning to get a white Bull Terrier, it is important to bear in mind that the breed does have an inherited predisposition to deafness. The genes for this condition come from both parents. Many breeders will have had their puppies tested for deafness. At six weeks of age, the puppies can be taken to a specialist centre that conducts the BAER test for deafness. Each puppy is tested individually, and each ear is tested to register how many decibels the puppy can hear. The puppies that pass the test are given a certificate, and this should be included in the paperwork when you buy a puppy.

It is important that puppies have a hearing test before they go to their new homes. *Photo: Alice van Kempen.*

You can test on the spot by making a loud noise behind an unsuspecting pup, such as clapping hands, ringing an alarm clock, squeaking a toy or clapping hands. This is not foolproof, however, as a dog can respond to movement, the reaction of others, and numerous other signs. The only way of really being sure is with a BAER test.

However, we tested and found one pup did not respond to anything we did. The morning she was due to go to the vet, she was playing in the garden when an extremely low-flying plane went over and crashed into the sea only half a mile away. Picking myself up from the rose bed where I had ducked down for safety, I inspected the house windows for damage – and then remembered the pup. She had

bolted home to the safety of her kennel. I assumed she must have reacted to the vibrations, but from that moment she could quite clearly hear. The bones in her ears had shaken open. Of course we kept testing her, not believing our luck. But she became quite capable of hearing a cellophane toffee wrapper being opened from the bottom of the garden!

This was a story with a happy ending, but think very carefully before taking on a Bull Terrier with hearing problems. A deaf Bully is such a risk to himself. Trainers advocate using hand signals to communicate. Yes, these work well – provided the dog is looking in your direction.

Accidents happen all too easily, and if you take on a deaf dog, you will need to be vigilant at all times.

I heard of a deaf Bull Terrier that was collected from a rescue centre and went to his new home where an elderly Bully was already in residence. After suspicious greetings, this relationship worked very well, with the deaf dog being guided by the elder. She would tell the youngster that dinner was ready or that the rats needed dealing with down in the stream. However, when the older dog died, the deaf dog became more accident-prone, and, on one occasion, the owner had to resuscitate the dog after he fell in

It is a good idea to go to a show so that you can see a variety of different Bull Terriers.

the deep part of the pond.

There are a few dedicated owners who can cope with living with a deaf dog, but you should think long and hard before taking on this extra responsibility.

FINDING A PUPPY

Once you have decided to bring a Bull Terrier into your life, you need to find one. Make sure you go to well-informed sources. If someone is giving you authoritative advice, ask when they last had a Bully – it is often never! These are dogs of distinction, thinking dogs, and their responses are through their intelligence rather than by rote. You should not entertain back-street breeders, pet shops or

puppy farms. Their stock is not necessarily cheaper; the pups may not be reared correctly and there may be health issues as a result of indiscriminate breeding.

Consult specialist dog publications, such as *Dog World, Our Dogs, Kennel Gazette,* and *Your Dog* in the UK, or the *American Kennel Gazette* or *Purebred Dogs* in the USA. You should also contact the Kennel Club of Great Britain or the American Kennel Club where you can find details of breed clubs in your area. There are 11 regional clubs in Great Britain, so you should be able to find one within a 100-mile radius. The club secretary will be able to tell you which breeders have

litters or are planning litters.

It is also a good idea to go to a dog show so you can see all ages, colours and sizes. There are club shows that are dedicated to Bull Terriers, or you can go to the big Championship shows, selecting the day that the Terrier Group is judged. Once at a show, talk to other visitors, watch the classes, and observe all the different makes and shapes. You may think one Bull Terrier is as handsome as another, but you are going to have your Bully for the next dozen years, so you want an animal that you can be proud of. Seeing Bull Terriers *en masse* gives you a chance to make sure you still want this particular breed.

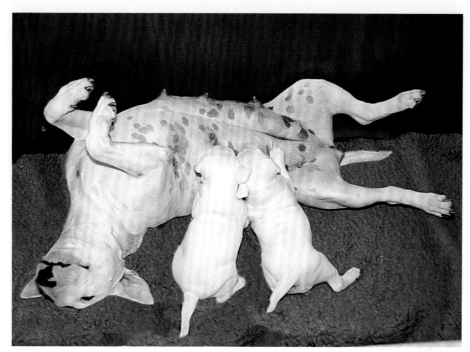

Bull Terrier bitches do not have big litters, so you may have to wait before a puppy becomes available.
Photo: Alice van Kempen.

THE WAITING GAME

When you have found a breeder who might suit your needs, make sure that in your preliminary discussions you explain exactly what sort of dog you want: i.e. a companion dog or a potential show dog. You will also need to describe the make-up of your household – whether you have children, other pets etc. – so the breeder will know which type of dog is most likely to suit your lifestyle. The breeder will also want to know what housing arrangements you plan for your puppy, and whether someone will be at home most of the time to care for the pup.

After talking to the breeder, you may be asked to put your name down on a waiting list. Bull Terriers average only four pups per litter, and there may be whelping or rearing problems. As a result, there are not vast numbers of pups available, so you should be prepared to wait until the breeder has the type of puppy you are looking for.

VIEWING THE PUPPIES

The first time you will be able to see the puppies is when they are two to three weeks of age. By this time, the pups should have overcome the trauma of being born. They should have settled tummies, their eyes will be open, and they will be ready to explore. If possible, take someone with you – not necessarily a Bull Terrier person,

but someone with an affinity with dogs who can give objective advice.

You will also get a chance to meet the dam of the litter and other close relatives, and this will give you an indication of the temperament that the puppies are likely to inherit. In most cases, the sire will not be resident, as breeders travel the length and breadth of the country to choose a stud dog that will complement their bitch's bloodlines. However, the breeder should have a photo of the sire, plus any other relevant information.

Take great care when you are inspecting the puppies – particularly if you have children with you. You will need to kneel

Make sure you see the mother with her puppies, as this will give you some idea of the temperament they are likely to inherit.

Photo: Alice van Kempen.

or crouch down if you want to hold a puppy so that it is no more than 30 cm (12 inches) from the ground. Puppies are wriggly creatures and accidents can happen all too easily. I had one visitor who dropped a pup from a metre high (3 ft) straight on to his back. Fortunately, the puppy landed on a layer of soft, thick, fleecy veterinary bedding, which cushioned the blow. If you have children, make them sit cross-legged on the floor so they can cuddle a puppy while holding it in a secure position.

Look for a lively, plump pup, not too long in the back, with a strong, sturdy rear end with well-bent stifle joints. Whippet-like, straight-legged back ends with long tails will nearly always remain that way. A strong back end is needed for the driving power capable for the task of powering the weighty adult. There is an expression, also used for a foal, stating that the youngster should be square, with a leg in each corner. When you see it, you will recognise the accuracy of the statement.

A tiny pup should be a solid little fellow. If there is any doubt on parentage (did the bitch carry out extra-curricular activity with the Labrador down the road?), the resultant pups will be floppy when picked up – like half-filled rubber hot-water bottles. I didn't really believe this until I whelped my son's Labrador and realised how different the little whelps (newborn pups) were from our own tough Bull Terriers.

It is important that the breeder knows your home circumstances to help you pick the right puppy. For example, if you are likely to be leaving the pup on his own for several hours at a time, the breeder will probably suggest you have a particularly happy, outgoing puppy, whereas a quiet, loving pup would be better suited to a

How do you decide which puppy to choose?

Watch the puppies play together and you will see their individual personalities start to emerge.
Photo: Alice van Kempen.

The breeder will help you assess which puppies have show potential.

home where he will spend most of his day being petted and cuddled.

SHOW PROSPECT

If you are looking for a puppy with show potential, you need to assess conformation, as well as markings on a white Bull Terrier.

Much importance is attached to a good mouth, but this cannot be clearly estimated until the Bull Terrier has grown up. The teeth change at four months and any obvious fault can be seen at this stage. Ideally, a four-month-old pup should have a top jaw well over the bottom one to allow for growth. In an adult dog, the aim is for the teeth to meet in a scissor bite, with the teeth on the upper jaw closely overlapping the teeth on the lower jaw.

If you are assessing a show prospect, look at the pup in profile. If he appears to be pouting with his bottom jaw as long as his top jaw, he is likely to be undershot. A badly undershot jaw is one that has grown longer in excess of the upper jaw. You can often place a two-pence coin on the extra length. An overshot jaw refers to the extra length of the upper jaw. However, this is more difficult to assess: when the pup grows at around four to six months, his egg-shaped profile becomes more emphasised by the top jaw rounding down and thus pulling the teeth in towards the lower jaw.

TAKING ON AN OLDER DOG

You may decide that you would like to miss out on the puppy phase and take on an older dog. There are many reasons why dogs need rehoming. An owner may become ill and be unable to manage his pets any longer; a job move or marital break-up are also common reasons for dogs going into 'rescue'. Unfortunately, there are also a percentage of cases where dogs have not been properly trained and cared for, and have become too much for their owners.

Bull Terriers are thinking dogs. If you find yourself asking a Bull Terrier: "What did you do that for, you silly dog?" then think it through from the dog's point of view and you will realise that he is being very clever. A dog left for many hours on his own has had time to think out all kinds of doggy plans. One rescue dog could open any sort of bolt and let himself out, or open the front door. We had to play him at his own game and think it out! All bolts are now at the top of the doors – not at dog height.

Taking on a rescued Bull Terrier can be a rewarding task, once you have got over the settling-in period and have learnt to understand your Bully. In most cases, you will know little of the dog's history and will have to find out what he is like. Is he a thief? If so, do not leave temptation in his way and put the chicken in the fridge until it is required. A cat chaser can be more difficult to solve.

You may decide that your lifestyle is better suited to taking on an older dog. *Photo: Alice van Kempen.*

No doubt your Bully will act the innocent when you are around, but as soon as you leave the room, the fun will begin!

One family had an old Great Dane and a rescued Bull Terrier who slept in the farmhouse rocking chair in front of the fire with the black cat. Harmony ensued as they enjoyed the warmth and companionship. But as soon as the dog and cat went outside, the Bull Terrier saw the cat as fair game and gave chase.

In most cases, an older dog will be a model of good behaviour for the first 10 days, and will then try every trick in the book to make his life as comfortable as possible. It is important to establish house rules so that your Bully understands what is acceptable behaviour. Try to stick to a routine, which will help your dog to settle into his new home.

THE NEW ARRIVAL

Chapter 4

Before you collect your puppy, much needs to be done in terms of preparing your home for the new arrival.

IN THE HOUSE

Some ground rules need to be established between all household members before you collect your puppy. Is the pup to be allowed to roam the entire house? Will you allow him upstairs, on the beds, or on the furniture where you usually sit? Do you plan to confine him to the kitchen or wherever his crate is located? No doubt some of these house rules will be broken once the newcomer has gained in confidence, so be flexible.

However, it is important to bear in mind that if you set your will against a Bull Terrier, he will win. Despite this, you must be seen as the boss, so try to avoid confrontation by thinking of another way around a given situation to ensure that harmony can be restored.

Decide where the feeding corner will be. A bigger dog has considerable bulk. If you try to push him out of the gangway when he is eating, you may be asking for trouble.

It is a good idea to erect a small gate (such as a baby stairgate) across the doorway of the kitchen or wherever your Bull Terrier is to be confined. You can then answer the front door without him slipping through your legs and running away down the road. The gate is also a good means of keeping dogs and noisy children separated; the children can lean over the gate to stroke and talk to the puppy, but there can be no rough and tumble.

A Bull Terrier will find amusement in all manner of household items: chewing electrical wires, swinging on long curtains, dragging a mat across the floor, pulling tablecloth corners and slithering around on slippery floor surfaces. Before your puppy arrives, try to view the house from his perspective and make it as dog-proof as possible.

IN THE GARDEN

Safety should be your main aim. You have an expensive and precious commodity, the envy of many. Not only do you need to ensure the dog cannot get out of the premises but that thieves cannot get in! Most important is to have a secure garden with strong fencing at least 1.22 metres (4ft) high. Thin lap wood fencing is of no use at all – one Bull Terrier was seen disappearing through such a fence. If the garden is not well fenced, or has weak spots, a Bull Terrier may well wander.

If you are unable to fence the

A Bull Terrier puppy will explore his new environment, so you must ensure that it is safe and secure.   *Photo: Alice van Kempen.*

garden securely, it may be worth building a run from at least 1.22m (4ft) high mesh. The mesh needs to be made so that the occupant can see what is going on in the garden. Solid fences are too easy to climb – even a baton fixed horizontally along the top of the wire is too inviting. Once a Bully gets his paws on it, he then uses his powerful shoulders and is up and away!

Climbing out of the run can be a dog's determined ambition. If he has been left on his own, whatever else is there to do? So if

you are building a run for an adult, it may be worth considering roofing it with more mesh.

A crate or kennel placed inside the run gives the dog a place to rest at various times through the day. The run should also have a waterproof cover over at least part of it, to provide shelter should the wind cause a draught or if it starts raining. The run needs to be large enough for an adult to be able to relieve himself when necessary without being in the immediate vicinity of his

sleeping arrangements. It is important to pick up in the run and clean it at regular intervals.

If your Bully is allowed the run of the garden, be prepared for his help. The bulbs you planted yesterday will be dug up ready for you today! The greenhouse is a favourite exploring zone – plastic pots can be made to fly all over the garden – and when your Bully gets bored, he can nip off the blooms from your favourite flowers. Forewarned is forearmed!

When buying fertilizers and pesticides, read the packet! Some say 'safe for children and pets'; others do not mention them. Plants that are sprayed for various diseases can harm your puppy and have disastrous results. There are some sprays that are dangerous for a puppy's feet, as their pads are not hardened up sufficiently. Ideally, avoid using sprays of any type unless you are 100 per cent confident that they are non-toxic to animals. It is also important to check if there are any plants in your garden (or houseplants in your home) that are poisonous to dogs. You can find out this information via the internet, or by asking for advice at your local garden centre.

SHOPPING LIST
There are a few essential items you will need to buy in order to care for your puppy.

CRATE
A sturdy crate with good hinges and latches is a worthwhile investment. You will need to buy

a crate that is big enough to accommodate an adult Bull Terrier and will allow him to stand up or to lie down, stretched out. An ideal size is 90 cm by 60 cm by 60 cm (35.5 x 23.5 x 23.5 inches).

A cardboard box with one side cut down to 15 cm (6 inches), placed at the back of the crate, will serve as an excellent bed for the first few nights and can easily be replaced if found chewed to bits in the morning. Alternatively, you can buy a puppy-size non-chewable oval plastic bed, which will keep the chilly floor draughts off the pup.

The crate needs a layer of newspaper to line the base. Place bedding in the dog bed or cardboard box. As the pup grows, you can dispense with the bed and line the crate with bedding. The best type of bedding is synthetic fleece, which allows moisture to drain through to the newspaper below. It is also easy to wash and dry. If synthetic fleece is not available, a folded blanket will provide warmth. Smooth it down but leave a little (6 cm/2.5 in) up each side so that the pup has something soft to lean against. A loose piece of blanket in the

The Bull Terrier is very adaptable and if he is accustomed to a crate from an early age, he will be happy to settle in it.

cage should be available for him to snuggle up to, acting as a substitute for his brothers and sisters.

A cover, a blanket or similar can be thrown over the crate to provide a more secure environment. I do not favour a plastic cover, as the pup will instantly make it his life's endeavour to chew and swallow it. I have a Bull Terrier who pulled an entire double size duvet through an 8 cm (3 in) wire square in his cage. He was found fast asleep and very cosy, thank you!

The crate door should be left open, when you can supervise him, so that the puppy can learn that this bed is his safe area. At

no time must the crate be considered as a prison. Ten minutes is usually sufficient time to get the lunch dished up, or some other event for which the dog would be safer out of the way. By using a crate as a bed, the dog learns that he is safe and secure, even when he is in the car or at a show.

Many pet owners do not like the idea of crating their dogs – neither do breeders if a dog is to spend most of the day shut in. But, in reality, a dog may go for months without having the crate door shut. But the crate provides a safe haven at times when you cannot supervise your puppy. All our dogs look upon their crates as their indoor beds and the elderly dogs can enjoy a peaceful sleep with the door closed, knowing that any cheeky youngster cannot sneak up on them unawares.

Don't forget to make sure that the crate will fit in the car. Also ensure that the door is the right way round for getting the dog in and out without having to get the entire crate out, which is not very convenient if you have stopped in a lay-by for 10 minutes to let your dog have a short relief break!

You need to buy a feeding bowl that can stand up to a fair amount of wear and tear.

FOOD

The breeder will give you details of the diet that the puppies are being fed so you can buy in a supply. In fact, most breeders will give you a small amount of food to tide you over the first few days. It is very important not to change diet when the puppy is moving home, as it will result in digestive upset. A change of water from one part of the country to another is enough to cause an upset tummy at this vulnerable time.

DISHES

You will need two dishes: one for food and one for water. Stainless-steel dishes are suitable and can stand up to Bull Terrier teeth. The dishes are often turned upside down and treated as a skateboard on the concrete or floor tiles. Plastic bowls must never be used, as they will be chewed. The pieces that break off have the sharpest of points and edges, and are very dangerous, especially if swallowed. You can also buy a bowl with a bracket attached to it, which is then fitted to the inside of a crate.

Bull Terriers are messy drinkers; they tend to dribble the last mouthful back, making a puddle around the bowl. A useful trick to keep your carpet flooring dry is to sink a medium-sized water bowl into a larger one so that there is a ledge to catch the splashes.

Some dogs like to lift their bowls up and carry them to another part of the room. One of our Bull Terriers would carry his supper to his bed, where he could enjoy it in peace!

COLLARS AND LEADS

The first collar you buy for your puppy should be lightweight and made of nylon. You can graduate to a stronger web collar when he is older. The Bull Terrier has a knack of making his neck short and fat when you are measuring him for a collar; then, once you have purchased the collar, his head becomes long and thin so he can play the game of slipping his collar!

A nylon slip-lead should be used for the first time you try out a lead. These are used in the show ring and can be slipped on when a puppy is busy playing. They are very lightweight and so minimise the feeling of restraint.

An extending lead is a useful purchase when your Bull Terrier is a little older. This type of lead can be used if you are walking on land that is close to the road, or if you want to prevent your Bully from having too much freedom – for example, if you are walking on a beach and your Bully is intent of chasing seagulls.

It is sensible to practise using an extending lead in a controlled area to begin with. It takes a bit of practice, but, in time, you can use the control to send messages down the lead when you are standing at some distance. Half a press on the control makes the dog realise you are going to stop in a moment, and he can slow up and even wait for you to catch up.

ID

Your Bull Terrier should wear some form of ID in case he ever gets lost. This can be a metal tag attached to his collar, or you can get your telephone number embroidered on to his collar. It is also advisable to invest in a permanent form of ID, such as a tattoo or a microchip.

A hollow rubber toy or Kong will help to keep your Bull Terrier occupied – particularly if it is filled with food...

TOYS

A large-size rubber Kong can provide endless pleasure for a Bull Terrier. Squeaky toys are even more fun, but your dog will need to be supervised, as these toys are made of a soft plastic, which is easily torn and swallowed, including the squeaker.

DANGER!

It is essential that your Bull Terrier is supervised at all times if he has a toy or a chew. I have already highlighted the danger of toys that can be chewed and swallowed – but this also applies to some chews. Nylabone chews are OK, as long as a dog is supervised, but do not buy cheap imitations.

There was one time when I was at a show and a Bull Terrier on a neighbouring bench was choking.

The owner was in the ring with a dog and left her other dog with a chew to keep him happy while she was away. I managed to hook my finger into his mouth and retrieve a yard of foaming chew. As the dog had not been able to bite pieces off the chew, he had tried swallowing it down instead. In this situation, leaving the Bull Terrier with a few dog biscuits would be far more suitable.

You may think you are providing your Bull Terrier with a treat if you give him a bone, but if you do you need to be very careful. Bones can splinter and cause injuries if they are swallowed. For this reason, avoid cooked bones, which splinter more easily, and always supervise your Bull Terrier when he has a bone.

provide for your Bull Terrier must be large enough not to be swallowed.

FINDING A VET

Before you bring your puppy home, book an appointment with a vet for a health check. Do some homework and find a veterinary practice that will be suitable for your Bull Terrier. Find out if vets in the practice are familiar with the breed, and also ask what facilities are available.

At the first appointment, the vet can give your pup a thorough check-up, and you will be given advice on worming regimes and when to start the all-important vaccination programme. See Chapter Eight: Happy and Healthy.

COLLECTING YOUR PUPPY

A puppy is ready to go to his new home at seven to eight weeks of age. At six weeks, the mother will search for her puppies, but at eight weeks she will come out to the car and positively wave them goodbye. She will then find her ball and be off to play on her own. In the wild she would return to the rest of the adult pack at this time, having completed her maternal duties.

If possible try to collect your pup in the morning so that he is wide-awake and full of adventurous bravado. You will arrive home in daylight and the new environment looks exciting rather than full of intimidating shadows.

The breeder will have prepared some essential items in a puppy

The breeder will allow the puppies to go their new homes when they are around eight weeks of age.

My red Bull Terrier died of stoppage (blockage in the intestines), not from a bone, but from corn-on-the-cob. He stole the husk from the dustbin and gulped it down in three bites. He had a prize and was not going to let his other four-legged pals have any of it. Three months later, he was rushed to the vet with stoppage. Too late! The vet investigated and a half-inch object was found. It had left the dog's stomach and moved in the intestine and jammed. One of the veterinary nurses recognised the pattern on the object – the diamond shape of a corn on the cob husk.

Equally, all the toys you

REMEMBER THE PAPERWORK

Paperwork must change hands. This will generally include the following:

- Kennel Club registration papers for transfer of ownership. If the breeder has already registered the names of the pups with the Kennel Club, you can complete the transfer. If not, you should complete the form and send the transfer, duly signed by you and by the breeder, together with the fee.

- A pedigree, which is your puppy's family tree. It should go back at least three generations.
- An inoculation certificate if the pup has been vaccinated.
- Tattooing or microchip evidence.
- BAER test hearing certificate.
- A diet sheet, which should give details of feeding from puppyhood through to adulthood.
- Details of worming treatment to date.

pack. These will include a small supply of food so the puppy does not have to cope with a change of diet in the first few days. Some breeders will provide a piece of blanket that has been with the litter for a day. This will have familiar smells of Mum and security, and will help to reassure the pup that all is well.

THE JOURNEY HOME
It is tempting to want to nurse and cuddle your pup on the journey home, but it is safer if he is accommodated in a crate. Whoever the pup is going to belong to should sit by the crate and care for the pup on the way home. This will ensure that you are the link between his old world and his new world – and this bond will last for the puppy's lifetime.

Arriving in a new home is a daunting experience, even for the most confident puppy. *Photo: Alice van Kempen.*

Introduce your puppy to the new members of his family, but try to keep proceedings as calm as possible.

Photo: Alice van Kempen.

MEETING THE FAMILY

Everyone in the family will be desperate to meet the new arrival, but it is important to bear in mind that arriving in a strange environment is a daunting experience for a new puppy. Try to keep proceedings as calm as possible. Introduce each member of the family one at a time and at floor level so the puppy does not feel intimidated. Talk to the puppy in a kindly tone of voice to give him reassurance.

If you have children, you should teach them how to behave around a puppy before your Bully comes home. Place the puppy in the child's lap when he/she is sitting and encourage the child to stroke the puppy between his ears, approaching from the side rather than reaching over his face.

MEALTIMES

Your puppy will probably need four meals a day when he first arrives home. If he is reluctant to eat to begin with, do not be alarmed. A pup has so much to get used to in his new home, he may temporarily lose his appetite. Give him a chance to eat, and take away the leftovers after 10 minutes. At the next meal, present him with a fresh bowl of food. A Bully loves his food, and your puppy will soon be clearing his bowl with lightning speed.

HOUSE TRAINING

If your pup has been living with his mother, he will have learnt to keep the bed dry and use the newspaper on the surrounding floor. He will have watched his mother going outside to relieve herself, but he may not have grasped the principle of being clean. However, if you establish a routine and are vigilant, your puppy will soon get the idea.

Remember that a pup needs to relieve himself every two hours, as well as after a meal, a drink, a play session or a sleep. Carry your puppy to the area in the garden that you wish him to use in adult life, and give him a chance to have a sniff and explore the area. When he performs, be lavish with the praise.

A hint here – don't select a spot immediately outside the back door (which is tempting if it is pouring with rain). The dog will favour this area for the rest of his life – and it is just where you wish to walk!

Try to space out your puppy's meals out as widely as is convenient over the day. At eight to 10 weeks, puppies learn quicker than at any other time, and it will not be long before he gets the message.

THE FIRST NIGHT

After a day exploring his new home, your puppy will be exhausted – but that does not

Take your puppy out to the garden at regular intervals, and he will soon learn what is required. *Photo: Alice van Kempen.*

mean that he will sleep through the night! He will not be used to sleeping on his own and he will miss the comfort and warmth of his littermates.

The best plan is to make the crate as cosy as possible, with a cardboard box or bed lined with bedding, and, if possible, the piece of blanket smelling of his brothers and sisters. You can also provide a half-filled hot-water bottle, making sure it is very well wrapped. Some owners place a loud ticking alarm clock in the room to add a comforting noise; we have a radio turned on low so that the pup does not feel so lonely.

Before you put your puppy in the crate, feed a meal as per the breeder's diet sheet and the pup

should doze off quite quickly. The problem is that, in time, he will wake up and cry and howl when he discovers that the house is eerily quiet. There are two courses of action: you can let him cry it out, or you can take the crate upstairs into your bedroom so he has some companionship. Do not take him into your bed, as it will form a bad habit and makes it harder the next night to accept the downstairs apartment. Although you do not want to reward his cries with your presence, you have to balance this with the needs of the rest of the household. You will find that as soon as your puppy has learnt to look on his crate as his own special den, he will be happy to settle in it.

HANDLING

It is important that your puppy gets used to being handled at an early age.

Pick up each paw in turn.

Open the mouth so you can check teeth and gums.

Check the ears.

EARLY LESSONS

It is your job to train your Bull Terrier puppy to become a well-adjusted adult. Lessons can start from the moment your puppy arrives in his new home, when he will be getting used to an unfamiliar environment. This is particularly the case if your puppy has been reared in a kennel rather than in the breeder's home.

Initially your puppy needs to become accustomed to household noises from washing machines to vacuum cleaners. Television can be fascinating, with flashes of colour and unexpected noises. When your pup is slightly older he will be able to see the shapes as people and animals. Horseracing is the favourite among our dogs.

HANDLING

Each evening make an opportunity for the pup to be petted and to play with members of the household. He can be stroked and handled all over, which will help when he needs to be groomed or examined by the vet. You can also take the opportunity to open his mouth and inspect his teeth. Lift up each paw and check the nails. If your puppy is used to this, he will learn to accept having his teeth cleaned and his nails trimmed (see Chapter Five: The Best of Care).

The Bull Terrier's erect ears are a distinctive feature of the breed, but they may go through some funny stages as a puppy matures. A puppy's ears gradually come

The age at which a puppy's ears become erect may vary.

up on to the top of their heads, which is the correct ear set. The ears start unfolding from 10 days onwards; they seem to come up sideways and, at about eight weeks old, have started to bring up the flap to form an upright trumpet. These flaps bounce up and down in a cute fashion, but they become stronger by three months old.

Once the puppy starts changing his teeth, they may flop down again. If the earflaps are particularly heavy, they may be too much for the blood vessels to hold upright, and, as the dog gets bigger, they may need help. Massaging the ears can become part of the evening cuddle routine in the hope of sufficiently strengthening the blood vessels. If you have

concerns about your puppy's ear carriage, consult the breeder, as he or she may be able to offer additional advice.

WEARING A COLLAR

The breeder may have put collars on the puppies, but this is not always the case. The best plan is to put the collar on immediately before a mealtime so that the pup has something to think about other than the collar. You can also put it on when the puppy is sleeping on your lap, when he will not really notice it. The collar should only be left on for short periods. It should provide just enough restraint around his neck for him to realise that something is controlling him. Never leave your puppy unattended with the

As soon as your Bull Terrier has completed his vaccinations, the fun can start and you can venture out into the big wide world. *Photo: Alice van Kempen.*

collar on, as he may try scratching it off and could catch his claw in it.

CAR TRAVEL

Your puppy should be taken for short car rides, accommodated in a crate. Most Bull Terriers enjoy car travel, and will hop into the car at every opportunity. If your puppy is a little car sick to begin with, do not feed him before a car journey, and only travel for a short distance. If you drive to a park and give your pup a run, he will soon learn to associate the car with having fun and will get over his initial queasiness.

BASIC COMMANDS

There are certain instructions that a Bull Terrier should learn to obey instantly for his own safety and so that you can control his actions. The most urgent is that "No" means 'no'. When caught in the act of some misbehaviour, a clear disapproving note in your voice will give him the general idea that you disapprove of his actions. Your response must be instant. The dog will not link the punishment to the crime if you take him elsewhere before telling him off. For more information, see Chapter Six: Training and Socialisation.

PLAYTIME

A favourite game is chasing a broom. This is good fun, but

Establish a routine, and your puppy will soon settle in his new home. *Photo: Alice van Kempen.*

your Bully must also learn to give it up, otherwise you can look forward to 10 or 12 years of confrontation every time you want to sweep up! I find the best solution is to have two brooms. Once the first one has been wrenched from my hand, I use the other!

GOING OUT AND ABOUT

It will be some weeks before your puppy has finished his vaccination course and is ready to mix with other dogs. However, you can start the process of getting him used to the outside world before this date. A passing car is interesting to watch when snuggled in your arms rather than from pavement level. The more experiences you can expose your puppy to at this stage, the more likely he is to react calmly to new experiences in later life. (For more information on socialisation, see Chapter Six.)

THE BEST OF CARE

The Bull Terrier has a very strong constitution, and his short coat does not need elaborate grooming. However, you only get back what you put in.

DIET AND NUTRITION

Dog food now comes in a wide variety of forms, from the BARF diet (Biologically Approved Raw Food) to canned and dried, as well as home-made, using a wide variety of ingredients. A dog needs a well balanced diet that includes all the essential nutrients. These are:

- **Proteins:** These contain the essential amino acids that all dogs need but they cannot make on their own.
- **Fats and fatty acids:** These come either from plants or animal sources. They provide energy and help to produce a good coat. In cold weather it is

It is essential that a growing puppy has a well-balanced diet. *Photo: Alice van Kempen.*

It is important to consider your Bull Terrier's energy requirements when planning a diet.
Photo: Alice van Kempen

a good idea to increase the fat content of the diet, especially for animals that are kennelled.

- **Carbohydrates:** These come in the form of starches, sugar and fibre. They also supply energy for the dog, and are usually supplied from cereal or plants.
- **Vitamins:** These are essential to the well being of the dog. Do not give more than recommended, as over-supplementation can cause

problems. For example, excess vitamin A in the system can cause bone and joint pain, brittle bones and dry skin, and too much D can give problems with bone development.

- **Minerals:** These are very important, but are only needed in the smallest amounts. It is not easy to get the ratio of these correct, so do follow the directions on the container very carefully. For example: calcium

and phosphorus are needed for healthy bones and teeth, but too much can cause skeletal problems.

BARF DIET
The BARF or 'Biologically Appropriate Raw Food' diet is based on feeding raw food, which includes bones, eggs and vegetables. Only raw bones are fed, as they are easily digestible. Chicken wings and bodies are

**Home-made: You may prefer to feed
a more natural diet.**

**Complete feed: This fulfils all your dog's
nutritional requirements.**

very soft and easy to eat, although bodies are not easy to obtain. Marrowbones that have been sawn rather than chopped are also given. Additives, such as vitamins and probiotics, are sometimes used with this form of diet. Patties are also made with a mixture of minced bones, offal, fruit and vegetables, with eggs and oils being added. For more information you can read books on the BARF diet written by Dr. Ian Billinghurst.

This is a very natural way to feed a dog, and it often suits the Bull Terrier, as some can be prone to skin troubles.

HOME-MADE DIET
You can feed your Bull Terrier on a home-made diet. Protein will be needed from meat or fish, and you will need a mixer. You can make your own biscuits or buy a good-quality wholemeal biscuit.

Eggs, cheese and yoghurt are also good for a Bull Terrier. Fish can include tinned pilchards, with or without tomato sauce, or fresh fish if cooked in a pressure cooker for long enough for the bones to soften. Mackerel and herrings, being rich in oil, are particularly nutritious. Bones will need to be carefully removed from normally cooked fish.

Beef, chicken, lamb or tripe can all be used, though I can't imagine that cooking tripe in your kitchen will make you very popular! Beef can be fed raw, as can breast of lamb. When breast of lamb is cooked it can be rather greasy and not very appetising – and you will have to remove all the bones. You will find that your dog does very well on good-quality raw meat, but a mixer must be used, as a diet of just pure flesh will not contain all the elements needed to keep your dog healthy.

COMMERCIAL DOG FOOD
Commercial dog food comes in three different types: dry, moist and canned.

DRY
Also known as complete food, this type of diet is made with animal protein and/or cereal sources. It can be served dry or moistened with water. This diet is known as 'complete' because it is fully balanced and needs no additives.

A complete diet is easy to use and there are so many types available, you should be able to find one to suit your dog. Beware of complete diets that are very high in protein, as these do not always suit Bull Terriers.

Do follow the directions for use, and make sure fresh water is available at all times.

MOIST
Semi-moist food is usually sold

A puppy will need four meals a day when he first arrives in his new home.

You will need to keep increasing the amount of food while your puppy is still growing.

in sachets; they are not often used among Bull Terrier owners but can be useful in tempting a faddy feeder. They are usually only found in small sachets and seem to be directed towards the smaller breeds of dog.

CANNED
This is fed with a carbohydrate mixer; you can often buy a mixer made by the company producing the canned food. This type of diet is very appetising, and a shy feeder or convalescing dog will often eat it readily. Some Bull Terrier owners find that canned food can give their dogs flatulence, and it is not always popular for this reason.

PUPPY DIET
When you pick up your puppy from the breeder you will be given a diet sheet. Do try to stick with this; moving home is a very stressful time for a puppy so follow the breeder's advice for a couple of weeks at least. If you do need to change the diet, do so very slowly over two or three weeks, just adding a small amount of the new food every day.

A puppy needs four meals a day. Mealtimes can be scheduled at your convenience, but a rough guide would be 8am, midday, 4pm, and the last feed at 8pm. When a complete diet is being fed, some people leave a bowl of food down for the puppy to eat as and when he wants. However, if you have a very greedy puppy, this is not always ideal.

If you are feeding a complete diet, study the ingredients and follow the directions carefully.

You do not need to choose a diet with the highest protein but you do need a reasonable amount of oil/fat. The aim is for steady growth – you don't want a sumo wrestler at eight months.

The more traditional way of feeding a puppy is with two meat and two cereal meals a day. The meat meals consist of beef cut up in small pieces, plus a small amount of soaked wholemeal biscuit. The cereal meals are made up of puppy porridge with egg and goats' milk. Live yoghurt is a useful good addition.

Let the puppy eat as much as he wants and remove any food that is not eaten. A puppy should look nicely rounded, but not so full that he can hardly walk. Some will eat to excess if they are allowed. You will find that a puppy will go off the milky food first and you can drop one of the feeds around four and a half months and be down to two meals at six months.

The adolescent Bull Terrier needs more food than the adult, so keep increasing the food slowly. This may seem obvious but I have known people who just keep giving what the breeder has told them, not thinking to give more.

Young dogs, especially, can take a long time to body up. Two good meals a day are recommended, plus plenty of exercise. This helps to produce muscle rather than fat; fit not fat should be aimed for. The show dog is often rather too well

It is best to divide your adult Bull Terrier's food rations into two meals a day.

covered – you should be able to feel the ribs but not see them.

ADULT DIET
When a Bull Terrier is mature, at around two years of age, he will need less food. An adult Bull Terrier will enjoy two meals a day: a small snack in the morning and the main meal in the evening, or the other way about, whichever is most convenient.

Some dogs seem to put on weight on very little food and others will need a lot more, so you may have to adjust the amount you are feeding to keep your dog in good condition. Beware that a Bull Terrier will do his best to train you to feed him what he likes best, and it can be quite difficult to resist being coerced into changing the diet. However, a bit of pampering is not too harmful, as written by someone who has had to cook extra sausages for breakfast every morning...

If you own more than one Bull Terrier, you will probably find that they will need to be fed in different rooms. A dog that eats slowly will not appreciate a companion coming along to help out.

BONES AND CHEWS
Bones of the raw marrowbone variety are appreciated, but they should only be given under supervision. A Bull Terrier's jaws are very strong and a dog may bite off awkward-sized pieces. Large composite chews are very useful; most Bull Terriers like something to chew and the large ones are very good.

Rawhide chews need careful supervision; if a Bull Terrier can get a chew in his mouth, he will assume it can be swallowed, sometimes with disastrous consequences.

Pieces of raw fruit and vegetables are also very much enjoyed. We had a Bull Terrier

Your Bully will appreciate a bone, but make sure he is closely supervised.

WHAT NOT TO FEED

Some food is poisonous to dogs, so avoid the following:

- Chocolate (human variety)
- Fruit kernels
- Potato peelings and green potatoes
- Rhubarb leaves
- Mouldy/spoiled foods
- Alcohol
- Yeast dough
- Coffee grounds
- Hops (home brewing)
- Tomato leaves & stems
- Broccoli (large amounts)
- Raisins and grapes
- Cigarettes, loose tobacco, and cigars
- Onions.

This is by no means a fully comprehensive list, just some of the items often found around the home. Many house and garden plants are also not dog-friendly, so do be aware of what your puppy/adult is up to – many will try to eat almost anything.

who, while we were sitting down in the evening, would wander over to the fruit bowl and have a browse through, bring back her selected item, lie in front of the fire and take great enjoyment eating it. If it were an apple or pear, she would pull the stalk off and spit it out first!

SPECIAL DIETS.

Sometimes, due to medical conditions, special diets are needed and they can be very successful. Allergies can be a problem with Bull Terriers. Quite often a bland diet of chicken and rice is recommended with other feedstuffs added over a period of time so the food that is not tolerated can be identified and then eliminated.

DANGERS OF OBESITY

A fat dog is the fault of the owner; it is the owner that supplies the food. I know how difficult it is to keep the weight off Bullies, and have had my share of portly Bull Terriers.

Neutering does seem to lead to an increase of pounds, and you do feel very mean putting down a small bowl of food. However, providing the correct amount of food for your dog's needs, combined with extra exercise, will result in a lean and fit Bull Terrier. You can now buy low-calorie food for dogs, which can be beneficial when you are trying to reduce weight. Some veterinary practices run weight clinics for dogs, and a weekly weigh-in will keep you, and your Bull Terrier, on the right track.

A lean, fit Bull Terrier will suffer fewer health problems and will have an increased life expectancy. *Photo: Alice van Kempen.*

Being overweight puts an extra strain on the heart and joints, and exercise becomes problematical. It can also shorten the life expectancy of your Bull Terrier.

FEEDING REGIME

Our dogs have a small meal in the morning and their main meal in the evening, usually around half and hour after they get back from a walk, and at least an hour before we eat, just to keep the pecking order in the right place.

Because of the design of the head, some Bullies have a problem eating out of a bowl and are much happier having their food straight off the floor on a plastic mat. This can be washed after feeding.

Fresh water should be readily available. Remember to change the water several times a day. Some dogs make an awful mess in the water bowl, and if it is shared with more than one dog, the water will not stay fresh for long.

CHANGING DIETS

If you feel the need to change your Bull Terrier's diet for whatever reason, do so very slowly, adding a small amount of the new food, well mixed in with the old. In this way most stomach upsets should be avoided. Generally a Bull Terrier will be happy to eat new food, but it will take a while for his digestive system to get used to the new diet. Once you have a successful feeding regime, it is best to stay with it.

PUPPY EXERCISE

Initially a puppy will get as much exercise as he needs by playing in the garden.
Photo: Alice van Kempen.

Playing with a toy provides mental stimulation.

PUPPY EXERCISE

Puppies do not need a lot of exercise. If you have a large garden, a growing puppy will get all the exercise he needs simply by playing. Make sure you provide plenty of toys; car boot sales are a good place to pick up soft toys for a very reasonable price, and you can often get a large bag for a few pounds. Let the puppy play with a few toys at a <u>time</u>, and then bring out something new every now and again whilst putting the old toys in the wash. In this way, your puppy always has a 'new' toy to play with. Do keep an eye on what your puppy is getting up to when he plays with a toy; eyes and ears are easily removed as the puppy gets bigger and stronger.

Once your puppy has completed his vaccination course, you can go out for very short daily trips, with the pup on a lead. This should be no more than five minuets up the road and back, just for socialisation and to learn how to behave on a lead. Never take your puppy out straight after being fed, as he needs time to digest his food.

By six months you can start to go further on walks, but don't suddenly go for miles. A mile there and back is plenty to start with. For a young dog, two short walks are better than a marathon. Very gradually build up the exercise and don't forget to make it fun, with some roadwork and a good gallop if possible.

ADULT EXERCISE

An adult Bull Terrier will enjoy plenty of exercise. Three miles a day is fine with free running included, but most dogs are quite happy to do a lot more.

Do be aware of other people

ADULT EXERCISE
Photos: Alice van Kempen

A Bull Terrier will enjoy a daily walk with lots of interesting scents.

A run and a romp with a trustworthy companion is a bonus.

A Bully will appreciate a snooze on a cosy bed when he comes home.

Playing in the sea is a Bull Terrier favourite.

Photo: Alice van Kempen.

and dogs; we always put our Bullies on a lead if we see other dogs. If anything does happen, the Bull Terrier will get the blame, so try not to let yourself get in that position by keeping clear of other dogs if possible. We are very lucky in being able to exercise our dogs loose in the countryside, but we always keep a weather eye open for dogs, people and children – a Bully greeting is not for everybody.

You also need to be very careful with livestock in fields. Sheep are especially tempting to dogs, and a farmer is quite within his rights to shoot a dog that is worrying sheep.

When your Bully is full grown, you will need a well-fitting collar and a strong lead. The collar needs to be strong with a secure fastening, but try not to buy something that is very heavy to wear – you wouldn't want a heavy chain round your neck all day. Leather collars and leads are strong and look nice, but unfortunately they are also very appetising as far as a Bull Terrier is concerned. Nylon collars and leads are tough and durable, as long as they are not too narrow in width. I favour thick rope slip leads, which are easy to put on and are kind on the hands.

SWIMMING

Swimming is becoming a popular form of exercise for dogs, especially those recovering from injury. They can go to specially designed pools and be carefully monitored. We have had Bullies that would happily swim in our local river. I remember two swimming round the bend in the river, paddling away happily, side be side. It had me in quite a panic, as the banks get steep further downstream. Thankfully, they soon came into view, paddling back.

A Bull Terrier will also enjoy playing in the sea, and a good

An adult Bully can be very playful – particularly if he is the centre of attention.

gallop on the sands is very much appreciated. Remember to rinse the salt out of the coat afterwards – you can go prepared with a container of water and a towel or give a good rinse when you get home.

PLAYING GAMES

A Bull Terrier likes nothing better than getting your full attention and launching into a play session – it will usually be on his terms, but it is great fun all the same. Appearing with something stolen is often a favourite, and you are expected to chase after him until he gives in. Playing ball is enjoyed by some, but with others it's a case of 'if you want it, you

fetch it'. Rope toys are also very popular for tug games, but do be careful with puppies and their teeth. It is very easy to dislodge a baby tooth and it may cause the adult teeth to come through misplaced. You also need to bear in mind that a Bull Terrier is very strong, and if he tries to shake his tug toy, your teeth will rattle.

Footballs are also enjoyed; a Bully is very efficient at dribbling the ball very fast, and you are welcome to join in. Sadly, the ball can soon puncture, as a Bull Terrier is not known for being soft in the mouth. In order to prevent this happening, you can buy a ball with a webbing strap so the dog can carry it safely.

Hide-and-seek is another favourite game. You can teach your dog to search for hidden toys – and you will be surprised how quickly he learns the name of a toy – and bring back the correct one.

There is one game beloved by all Bullies, and that is a session of mad galloping. A Bull Terrier does not mind if he is in the house or the garden, all of a sudden he will take off at high speed, do an amazing turn in mid air, bounce off the wall, furniture or doors, and finish with several mad laps, taking rugs and chairs with him if he is in the house – all carried out with a wicked glint in his eyes.

GROOMING

The Bull Terrier has a low-maintenance coat, which requires no more than regular brushing.

GROOMING

With his short coat, a Bull Terrier does not need a lot of grooming. A brush with a horse dandy brush is good for cleaning off mud, and a mitt with rubber teeth is ideal for removing dead coat. A Bull Terrier moults twice a year; the heaviest moult is in the spring. Grooming at this time is particularly important, as it helps the new coat to come through and also lessens the hair around the home.

While you are grooming your Bully, it is a good idea to check him over. If a problem is diagnosed at an early stage, it is much easier to treat.

EYES

The eyes should be clean and bright. If the third eyelid is up or the eye is watering a lot, consult your vet. There may be a foreign body in the eye or it could be an infection – especially if the discharge is yellow or green.

EARS

The ears should be clean with no smell to them. Scratching the ears, head shaking, and/or an objectionable smell means a trip to the vet. It may be a foreign body in the ear. With their upright ears it is easy for grass seeds to get in or it may be ear mites. Haematomas can also appear almost overnight. They are hot, blood-filled blisters on the ears and do need veterinary treatment, but your pet may still end up with a cauliflower ear.

Don't delay consulting the vet if your Bull Terrier has ear problems, as they can take a long time to get better if the condition is allowed to worsen.

Quite often, a Bull Terrier will get a lot of scurf around the edges of his ears. If you apply some olive oil for a few days, and gently rub it in, it will usually loosen it and the scurf can then be carefully washed off using a little baby shampoo and cotton wool.

TEETH

Teeth must be checked on a regular basis. While your Bull Terrier is a puppy, keep an eye on his milk teeth. When a baby tooth comes out, the bleeding can be quite dramatic. You will need to check that it is only a tooth that has fallen out just to be on the safe side, but the

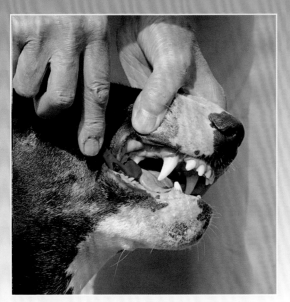

Teeth should be cleaned on a routine basis.

Trim the tip of the nails using nail clippers.

bleeding usually stops very quickly and the puppy is none the worse. While a puppy is teething, he will probably take a little longer over eating his food, but this is nothing to worry about. Sometimes the canines don't come out and the new tooth will grow against the old tooth. If it is firmly fixed, you may need your vet to remove it. If you are concerned about the teeth at any time, consult your vet.

Bull Terriers are very stoic about putting up with pain or discomfort. A Bully can have problems with his teeth and it is not until he is having difficulty with eating or has bad breath that you realise something is wrong. Misplaced canines are a common problem in the breed. The canine

teeth or tooth (and it can be just the one) will not be in the correct place and fit snugly on the outside of the upper jaw. Instead, the teeth will grow straight up into the roof of the mouth, and will cause nasty ulcers. Imagine having something sharp sticking in your mouth every time you closed. Your vet will be able to take the tip off the offending tooth and bring instant relief.

Carefully check the rest of the teeth for a build-up of tartar. You can buy toothbrushes and paste for dogs so you can routinely clean your Bull Terrier's teeth. Bones also do the job, but you still need to check the teeth regularly. If your Bull Terrier's teeth are in a bad state, you may need to book an appointment with the vet, who will be able to

scale and clean them while the dog is under anaesthetic.

FEET AND NAILS

A well-made foot will wear down the nails evenly, but poor feet, or exercising on soft ground, will allow the nails to grow too long. Nail clippers can be used, but take care not to take off too much, as you will cut into the quick and cause profuse bleeding. The result will be a very unhappy dog, and a battle next time you attempt the task. Just take off a little of the nail at a time; the quick is not easy to see in dark nails, so it is better to be safe than sorry. If nails are checked on a regular basis, a file is probably a better way to keep nails trim.

Don't forget the dewclaws, the

The white Bull Terrier will need regular bathing to keep his coat in top condition.   *Photo: Alice van Kempen.*

little nails just below the inside of the knee. Dewclaws may need trimming, as they grow very quickly; they tear easily and are very painful if damaged. Check the pads carefully for thorns or cuts, and if you have been out in the winter, wash the road salt off the feet, as they can get very sore.

BATHTIME
Baths are often needed for the white Bull Terrier. In warm weather you can do the job

using a couple of buckets of water and some dog shampoo. But do try to stand your dog on a hard surface; it is surprising how much mud you can churn up if you use the lawn.

In the cooler weather, you will need to retreat to the bathroom and use the bath. You will need three large towels, a bucket full of warm water, shampoo, and a large sponge, such as those used for washing cars. Once you have gathered the equipment, adopt the following procedure:

• Stand your dog in the bath and soak him thoroughly. Leave the head until last, as once that is wet he will start to shake.
• Work the shampoo into the coat and then rinse thoroughly.
• Place the bucket of water in the bath next to the taps so that it is easy to refill if necessary.
• The head should need no more than a quick rinse. If you do have to shampoo the

head, be careful with the
eyes.
- Use a towel to absorb most of
the moisture before your Bully
decides to shake.
- Wrap him in the towel and lift
him on to another towel
already spread on the floor.
- Rub him briskly all over – this
is the best part as far as your
dog is concerned.
- When he is nearly dry, finish
off with the last towel. Then
open the door and stand well
back!

BATHTIME TIPS
- Attaching a lead does help to
keep your Bull Terrier where
you want him – in the bath.
A wet Bully going round the
bathroom at full speed,
having escaped from the bath,
is a sight to behold. Catching
him is great fun, usually
resulting in a thorough
drenching for you and the
bathroom.
- Always use a shampoo
designed for dogs; you can get
special ones for dark dogs that

will help to prevent the scurf
rising to the top of the coat.
- After a bath, do keep your
Bull Terrier warm until he is
thoroughly dry.
- Watch carefully when your
Bull Terrier goes out into the
garden; there is nothing like a
bath to give a Bully an itchy
back. The only cure is a good
roll on the lawn, undoing all
your hard work, so be ready
to distract him with a treat or
a toy, or just take him outside
on a lead.

You need to be aware of the changing needs of your dog as he gets older.

Photo: Alice van Kempen.

CARING FOR THE OLDER DOG

An older Bull Terrier will usually enjoy his food, but he may need a softer diet that is lower in protein and is easier to digest. He may also take longer to eat his food. Little and often is appreciated, but do watch the quantities. A Bull Terrier is very adept at getting that extra treat and expanding his waistline.

Keep a close watch on his teeth, as they can cause a lot of misery. It is also worth going to the vet for regular MOTs. so that problems can be dealt with in the early stages.

Do make sure your oldie has a warm, cosy bed; he will feel the cold more as he gets older. Exercise should be at his own pace, perhaps a trip to favourite places in the car and a quiet walk when you arrive instead of a long walk to get there. Old Bull Terriers are wonderful and deserve the best.

LETTING GO

But when the time comes and life is becoming increasingly difficult for your old friend, do not let him linger in pain because you cannot bear to let him go. He has given you a lifetime of love and should not be allowed to suffer.

Arrange with your vet to come to your house, or take your Bully in the car to the vet. You can ask the vet to come out to your car to give the injection so there is

In time you will be able to look back and remember all the happy times you spent with your beloved Bull Terrier. *Photo: Alice van Kempen.*

minimum upset and disruption. Of course, you will be in floods of tears, but this is a duty of care that you owe to your Bull Terrier. You may wish to take him home and bury him in the garden, or you may be able to have him cremated and then keep the ashes as a special memorial.

Life will be very strange without your shadow, but, if at all possible, get a new dog as soon as you can. Your old friend will always have a place in your heart, but, in time, you will be compensated with having a new character to love.

TRAINING AND SOCIALISATION

Chapter 6

When you decided to bring a Bull Terrier into your life, you probably had dreams of how it was going to be: long walks together, cosy evenings with a Bully lying devotedly at your feet, and, whenever you returned home, there would always be a special welcome waiting for you.

There is no doubt that you can achieve all this – and much more – with a Bull Terrier, but like anything that is worth having, you must be prepared to put in the work. A Bull Terrier, regardless of whether it is a puppy or an adult, does not come ready trained, understanding exactly what you want and fitting perfectly into your lifestyle. A Bully has to learn his place in your family and he must discover what is acceptable behaviour.

We have a great starting point in that the Bull Terrier has an outstanding temperament. He is loving and affectionate; he has a wicked sense of humour, and wants nothing more than to be part of family activities. It is also important to bear in mind the strength, tenacity, determination and, at times, downright stubbornness of his Bulldog and terrier ancestors.

THE FAMILY PACK

Dogs have been domesticated for some 14,000 years, but, luckily for us, they have inherited and retained behaviour from their distant ancestor – the wolf. A Bull Terrier may never have lived in the wild, but he is born with the survival skills and the mentality of a meat-eating predator who hunts in a pack. A wolf living in a pack owes its existence to mutual co-operation and an acceptance of a hierarchy,

as this ensures both food and protection. A domesticated dog living in a family pack has exactly the same outlook. He wants food, companionship, and leadership – and it is your job to provide for these needs.

YOUR ROLE

Theories about dog behaviour and methods of training go in and out of fashion, but in reality, nothing has changed from the day when wolves ventured in from the wild to join the family circle. The wolf (and equally the dog) accepts a subservient place in the family pack in return for food and protection. In a dog's eyes, you are his leader, and he relies on you to make all the important decisions. This does not mean that you have to act like a dictator or a bully. You are accepted as a leader, without argument, as long as you have the right credentials.

Do you have what it takes to be a firm, fair and consistent leader?

The first part of the job is easy. You are the provider, and you are therefore respected because you supply food. In a Bull Terrier's eyes, you must be the ultimate hunter because a day never goes by when you cannot find food. The second part of the leader's job description is straightforward, but for some reason we find it hard to achieve. In order for a dog to accept his place in the family pack, he must respect his leader as the decision-maker. A low-ranking pack animal does not question authority; he is perfectly happy to see someone else shoulder the responsibility. Problems will only arise if you cut a poor figure as leader and the dog feels he should mount a challenge for the top-ranking role.

HOW TO BE A GOOD LEADER

There are a number of guidelines to follow to establish yourself in the role of leader in a way that your Bull Terrier understands and respects. If you have a puppy, you may think that you don't have to take this on board for a few months, but that would be a big mistake. Start as you mean to go on, and your pup will be quick to find his place in his new family.

- **Keep it simple:** Decide on the rules you want your Bull Terrier to obey and always make it 100 per cent clear what is acceptable, and what is unacceptable, behaviour.
- **Be consistent:** If you are not consistent about enforcing rules, how can you expect your Bull Terrier to take you seriously? There is nothing worse than allowing your Bully to jump up at you one moment and then scolding him the next time he does it because you were wearing your best clothes. As far as the Bull Terrier is concerned, he may as well try it on because he can't predict your reaction.
- **Make it fun:** You are the boss, but that doesn't mean it has to be "No", "No", "No" all the time! If you carry on like this, your Bully will quickly switch off his hearing aid and ignore you. Make training fun, and you will get your Bull Terrier's attention focused on you.
- **Get your timing right:** If you are rewarding your Bull Terrier, and equally if you are

reprimanding him, you must respond within one to two seconds otherwise the dog will not link his behaviour with your reaction (see page 84).

- **Read your dog's body language:** Find out how to read body language and facial expressions (see page 82) so that you understand your Bull Terrier's feelings and his intentions.
- **Be aware of your own body language:** When you ask your Bull Terrier to do something, do not bend over him and talk to him at eye level. Assert your authority by standing over him and keeping an upright posture. You can also help your dog to learn by using your body language to communicate with him. For example, if you want your dog to come to you, open your arms out and look inviting. If you want your dog to stay, use a hand signal (palm flat, facing the dog) so you are effectively 'blocking' his advance.
- **Tone of voice:** Dogs are very receptive to tone of voice, so you can use your voice to praise him or to correct undesirable behaviour. If you are pleased with your Bull Terrier, praise him to the skies in a warm, happy voice. If you want to stop him raiding the bin, use a deep, stern voice when you say "No".
- **Give one command only:** If you keep repeating a command, or keeping changing it, your Bull Terrier will think you are babbling and

Try a daily reminder of good manners, such as teaching your Bull Terrier not to barge through doors, to underline your leadership.

will probably ignore you. If your Bully does not respond the first time you ask, make it simple by using a treat to lure him into position, and then you can reward him for a correct response.

- **Daily reminders:** A young, exuberant Bull Terrier is apt to forget his manners from time to time, and an adolescent dog may attempt to challenge your authority (see page 95). Rather than coming down on your Bull Terrier like a ton of bricks when he does something wrong, try to prevent bad manners by daily reminders of good manners.

For example:
i   Do not let your dog barge ahead of you when you are going through a door.
ii Do not let him leap out of the car the moment you open the door (which could be potentially lethal, as well as being disrespectful).
iii Do not let him eat from your hand when you are at the table.
iv Do not let him 'win' a toy at the end of a play session and then make off with it. You 'own' his toys, and you must end every play session on your terms.

You need to understand your Bull Terrier's body language so that you can detect a sudden mind shift which might lead to trouble.

UNDERSTANDING YOUR BULL TERRIER

Body language is an important means of communication between dogs, which they use to make friends, to assert status, and to avoid conflict. You need to get on your dog's wavelength by understanding his body language and reading his facial expressions. This is important with all dogs, but it is vital with a Bull Terrier. If a Bully detects a challenge, he will take action. If you can read his body language, you can take control of potentially difficult situations.

As you get to know your Bull Terrier, you will understand his reactions and responses, but here is a general guide of how to read canine behaviour:

- A positive body posture and a wagging tail indicate a happy,

confident dog.
- A crouched body posture with ears back and tail down show that a dog is being submissive. A dog may do this when he is being told off or if a more assertive dog approaches him.
- A bold dog will stand tall, looking strong and alert. His ears will be forward and his tail will be held high.
- A dog who raises his hackles (lifting the fur along his topline) is trying to look as scary as possible. This may be the prelude to aggressive behaviour, but, in many cases, the dog is apprehensive and is unsure how to cope with a situation.
- A playful dog will go down on his front legs while standing on his hind legs in a bow position. This friendly invitation says: "I'm no threat; let's play."

- A dominant, aggressive dog will meet other dogs with a hard stare. If he is challenged, he may bare his teeth and growl, and the corners of his mouth will be drawn forward. His ears will be forward and he will appear tense in every muscle (see page 100).
- A nervous dog will often show aggressive behaviour as a means of self-protection. If threatened, this dog will lower his head and flatten his ears. The corners of his mouth may be drawn back, and he may bark or whine.
- Some dogs are 'smilers', curling up their top lip and showing their teeth when they greet people. This should never be confused with a snarl, which would be accompanied by the upright posture of a dominant dog. A smiling dog will have a

low body posture and a wagging tail; he is being submissive and it is a greeting that is often used when low-ranking animals greet high-ranking animals in a pack.

GIVING REWARDS

Why should your Bull Terrier do as you ask? If you follow the guidelines given above, your Bully should respect your authority, but what about the time when he is heading for the horizon or has found a really enticing scent? You need to build up a relationship of trust and loyalty so that your Bull Terrier sees you as the focal person in his life – someone he wants to respond to.

Obviously this takes time to establish, but the more attention you pay to your Bully, and the more involvement you have with him, the more likely he is to interact positively with you. It is also important to find out what is the biggest reward for your dog – in a Bull Terrier's case, it will nearly always be food – and to give him a treat when he does as you ask. For some dogs, the reward might be a play with a favourite toy, but, whatever it is, it must be something that your dog really wants.

When you are teaching a dog a new exercise, you should reward him frequently. When he knows the exercise or command, reward him randomly so that he keeps on responding to you in a positive manner. If your dog does something extra special, like leaving his canine chum mid-play

A Bully loves his cuddles, but you will need an extra incentive, such as a treat or a toy, to make headway with training.

in the park, make sure he really knows how pleased you are by giving him a handful of treats or throwing his ball a few extra times. If he gets a bonanza reward, he is more likely to come back on future occasions, because you have proved to be even more rewarding than his previous activity.

TOP TREATS

Some trainers grade treats depending on what they are asking the dog to do. A dog may get a low-grade treat, such as a piece of dry food, to reward good behaviour on a random basis, such as sitting when you open a door or allowing you to examine his teeth. But high-grade treats, which may be cooked liver, sausage or cheese, are reserved for training new exercises or for use in the park when you want a really good recall. Whatever type of treat you use, remember to subtract it from your Bull Terrier's daily ration. Fat Bull Terriers are lethargic, prone to health problems, and will almost certainly have a shorter life-expectancy. Reward your Bull Terrier, but always keep a check on his figure!

HOW DO DOGS LEARN?

It is not difficult to get inside your Bull Terrier's head and understand how he learns, as it is not dissimilar to the way we learn. Dogs learn by conditioning: they find out that specific behaviours produce specific consequences. This is known as operant conditioning or consequence learning. Consequences have to be immediate or clearly linked to the behaviour, as a dog sees the world in terms of action and result. Dogs will quickly learn if an action has a bad consequence or a good consequence.

Dogs also learn by association. This is known as classical conditioning or association learning. It is the type of learning made famous by Pavlov's experiment with dogs. Pavlov presented dogs with food and measured their salivary response (how much they drooled). Then he rang a bell just before presenting the food. At first, the dogs did not salivate until the food was presented. But after a while they learnt that the sound of the bell meant that food was coming, and so they salivated when they heard the bell. A dog needs to learn the association in order for it to have any meaning. For example, a dog that has never seen a lead before will be completely indifferent to it. A dog that has learnt that a lead means he is going for a walk will get excited the second he sees the lead; he has learnt to associate a lead with a walk.

BE POSITIVE

The most effective method of training dogs is to use their ability to learn by consequence and to teach that the behaviour you want produces a good consequence. For example, if you ask your Bull Terrier to "Sit", and reward him with a treat, he will learn that it is worth his while to sit on command because it will lead to something pleasurable. He is far more likely to repeat the behaviour, and the behaviour will become stronger, because it

THE CLICKER REVOLUTION

Karen Pryor pioneered the technique of clicker training when she was working with dolphins. It is very much a continuation of Pavlov's work and makes full use of association learning. Karen wanted to mark 'correct' behaviour at the precise moment it happened. She found it was impossible to toss a fish to a dolphin when it was in mid-air, when she wanted to reward it. Her aim was to establish a conditioned response so the dolphin knew that it had performed correctly and a reward would follow.

The solution was the clicker: a small matchbox-shaped training aid, with a metal tongue that makes a click when it is pressed. To begin with, the dolphin had to learn that a click meant that food was coming. The dolphin then

learnt that it must 'earn' a click in order to get a reward. Clicker training has been used with many different animals, most particularly with dogs, and it has proved hugely successful. It is a great aid for pet owners and is also widely used by professional trainers who teach highly specialised skills.

Teaching will be more effective if you find a training area that is free from distractions.

Alice van Kempen.

results in a positive outcome. This method of training is known as positive reinforcement, and it generally leads to a happy, co-operative dog that is willing to work, and a handler who has fun training their dog.

The opposite approach is negative reinforcement. This is far less effective and often results in a poor relationship between dog and owner. In this method of training, you ask your Bull Terrier to "Sit", and, if he does not respond, you deliver a sharp yank on the training collar or push his rear to the ground. The dog learns that not responding to your command has a bad consequence, and he may be less likely to ignore you in the future. However, it may well have a bad consequence for you, too. A dog that is treated in this way may associate harsh handling with the handler and become aggressive or fearful. Instead of establishing a pattern of willing co-operation, you are establishing a relationship built on coercion.

GETTING STARTED
As you train your Bull Terrier, you will develop your own techniques as you get to know what motivates him. You may decide to get involved with clicker training or you may prefer to go for a simple command-and-reward

Make training fun, interspersing lessons with play.
Alice van Kempen.

formula. It does not matter what form of training you use, as long as it is based on positive, reward-based methods.

There are a few important guidelines to bear in mind when you are training your Bull Terrier:

- Find a training area that is free from distractions, particularly when you are just starting out.
- Keep training sessions short. Young puppies have very short attention spans, and older dogs will switch off if they are asked to do anything dull and repetitious.
- Do not train if you are in a bad mood or if you are on a tight schedule – the training session will be doomed to failure.
- If you are using a toy as a reward, make sure it is only available when you are

training. In this way it has an added value for your Bull Terrier.

- If you are using food treats, make sure they are bite-sized and easy to swallow; you don't want to hang about while your Bully chews on his treat.
- All food treats must be deducted from your Bull Terrier's daily food ration.
- When you are training, move around your allocated area so that your dog does not think that an exercise can only be performed in one place.
- If your Bull Terrier is finding an exercise difficult, try not to get frustrated. Go back a step and praise him for his effort. You will probably find he is more successful when you try again at the next training session.
- Always end training sessions on

a happy, positive note. Ask your Bully to do something you know he can do – it could be a trick he enjoys performing – and then reward him with a few treats or an extra-long play session.

In the exercises that follow, clicker training is introduced and followed, but all the exercises will work without the use of a clicker.

INTRODUCING A CLICKER
This is dead easy, and your ever-hungry Bull Terrier will learn about the clicker in record time! It can be combined with attention training, which is a very useful tool and can be used on many different occasions.

- Prepare some treats and go to an area that is free from

distractions. When your Bull Terrier stops sniffing around and looks at you, click and reward by throwing him a treat. This means he will not crowd you, but will go looking for the treat. Repeat a couple of times. If your Bully is very easily distracted, you may need to start this exercise with the dog on a lead.

- After a few clicks, your Bull Terrier understands that if he hears a click, he will get a treat. He must now learn that he must 'earn' a click. This time, when your Bully looks at you, wait a little longer before clicking, and then reward him. If your Bull Terrier is on a lead but responding well, try him off the lead.
- When your Bull Terrier is working for a click and giving you his attention, you can introduce a cue or command word, such as "Watch". Repeat a few times, using the cue. You now have a Bull Terrier that understands the clicker and will give you his attention when you ask him to "Watch".

TRAINING EXERCISES

You may not wish to become involved in formal training sessions, but you can use opportunities presented throughout the day to teach and reinforce the behaviour you want. For example, you can teach your Bull Terrier to "Sit" when you are presenting his food bowl, or you can tell him to "Wait" or "Stay" when you are getting him out of the car.

THE SIT

This is the easiest exercise to teach, so it is rewarding for both you and your Bull Terrier.

- Choose a tasty treat and hold it just above your puppy's nose. As he looks up at the treat, he will naturally go into the Sit. As soon as he is in position, reward him.
- Repeat the exercise, and when your pup understands what you want, introduce the "Sit" command.
- You can practise at mealtimes by holding out the bowl and waiting for your dog to sit. Most Bull Terriers learn this one very quickly!

With practice, your Bully will respond to the verbal command "Sit" and you can reward him on a random basis.

Use a treat to lure your Bull Terrier into the Down.

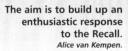

The aim is to build up an enthusiastic response to the Recall.
Alice van Kempen.

THE DOWN

Work hard at this exercise because a reliable Down is useful in many different situations, and an instant Down can be a lifesaver.

- You can start with your dog in a Sit, or it is just as effective to teach it when the dog is standing. Hold a treat just below your puppy's nose and slowly lower it towards the ground. The treat acts as a lure, and your puppy will follow it, first going down on his forequarters and then bringing his hindquarters down as he tries to get the treat.

- Make sure you close your fist around the treat, and only reward your puppy with the treat when he is in the correct position. If your puppy is reluctant to go Down, you can apply gentle pressure on his shoulders to encourage him to go into the correct position.
- When your puppy is following the treat and going into position, introduce a verbal command.
- Build up this exercise over a period of time, each time waiting a little longer before giving the reward, so the puppy learns to stay in the Down position.

THE RECALL

It is never too soon to start training the Recall. Make sure you are always happy and excited when your Bull Terrier comes to you, even if he has been slower than you would like. Your Bully must believe that the greatest reward is coming to you.

- You can start teaching the Recall from the moment your puppy arrives home. He will naturally follow you, so keep calling his name, and rewarding him when he comes to you.
- Practise in the garden, and when your puppy is busy

SECRET WEAPON

You can build up a strong Recall by using another form of association learning. Buy a whistle, and when you are giving your Bully his food, peep on the whistle. You can choose the type of signal you want to give: two short peeps, or one long whistle, for example. Within a matter of days, your dog will learn that the sound of the whistle means that food is coming.

Now transfer the lesson outside. Arm yourself with some tasty treats and the whistle. Allow your Bull Terrier to run free in the garden, and, after a couple of minutes, use the whistle. The dog has already learnt to associate the whistle with food, so he will come towards you. Immediately reward him with a treat and lots of

praise. Repeat the lesson a few times in the garden so you are confident that your dog is responding before trying it in the park. Make sure you always have some treats in your pocket when you go for a walk, and your dog will quickly learn how rewarding it is to come to you.

exploring, get his attention by calling his name. As he runs towards you, introduce the verbal command "Come". Make sure you sound happy and exciting, so your puppy wants to come to you. When he responds, give him lots of praise.
- If your puppy is slow to respond, try running away a few paces or jumping up and down. It doesn't matter how silly you look: the key issue is to get your puppy's attention – and then make yourself irresistible!
- In a dog's mind, coming when called should be regarded as the best fun because he knows he is always going to be rewarded. Never make the

mistake of telling your dog off, no matter how slow he is to respond, as you will undo all your previous hard work.

If you have built up a good Recall, you may want to free-run your dog – but you must be very careful with the location you choose. A Bull Terrier may get on well with other dogs, but you cannot control the dogs he meets. If your Bully feels threatened or challenged, you cannot answer for the consequences, and if he is off-lead, you have no control. If you are in a location where there is a strong chance of meeting other dogs, you are better off exercising your Bull Terrier on an extending lead.

TRAINING LINE
This is the equivalent of a very long lead, which you can buy at a pet store, or you can make your own with a length of rope. The training line is attached to your Bull Terrier's collar and should be around 15 feet (4.5 metres) in length.

The purpose of the training line is to prevent your Bull Terrier from disobeying you so that he never has the chance to get into bad habits. For example, when you call your Bully and he ignores you, you can immediately pick up the end of the training line and call him again. By picking up the line, you will have attracted his attention, and if you call in an excited, happy voice, your Bully will come to you. The

When your Bully is walking with you, there should be minimum tension on the lead.

moment he comes to you, give him a tasty treat so he is instantly rewarded for making the 'right' decision.

The training line is very useful when your Bull Terrier becomes an adolescent and is testing your leadership. When you have reinforced the correct behaviour a number of times, your dog will build up a strong recall and you will not need to use a training line.

WALKING ON A LOOSE LEAD

This is a simple exercise, which baffles many Bull Terrier owners. In most cases, owners are too impatient, wanting to get on with the expedition rather that training the dog how to walk on a lead. Take time with this one; the Bull Terrier is a very strong dog, and a Bully that pulls on the lead is no pleasure to own.

- In the early stages of lead training, allow your puppy to

pick his route and follow him. He will get used to the feeling of being 'attached' to you, and has no reason to put up any resistance.

- Next, find a toy or a tasty treat and show it to your puppy. Let him follow the treat/toy for a few paces, and then reward him.
- Build up the amount of time your pup will walk with you, and, when he is walking nicely by your side, introduce the verbal command "Heel" or "Close". Give lots of praise when your pup is in the correct position.
- When your pup is walking alongside you, keep focusing his attention on you by using his name, and then rewarding him when he looks at you. If it is going well, introduce some changes of direction.
- Do not attempt to take your puppy out on the lead until you have mastered the basics at home. You need to be confident that your puppy accepts the lead and will focus his attention on you, when requested, before you face the challenge of a busy environment.
- As your Bull Terrier gets bigger and stronger, he may try to pull on the lead, particularly if you are heading somewhere he wants to go, such as the park. If this happens, stop, call your dog to you, and do not set off again until he is in the correct position. It may take time, but your Bull Terrier will eventually realise that it is more

productive to walk by your side than to pull ahead.

STAYS

This may not be the most exciting exercise, but it is one of the most useful. There are many occasions when you want your Bull Terrier to stay in position, even if it is only for a few seconds. The classic example is when you want your Bull Terrier to stay in the back of the car until you have clipped on his lead. Some trainers use the verbal command "Stay" when the dog is to stay in position for an extended period of time, and "Wait" if the dog is to stay in position for a few seconds until you give the next command. Other trainers use a universal "Stay" to cover all situations. It all comes down to personal preference, and as long as you are consistent, your dog will understand the command he is given.

You can back up a verbal command with a hand signal when you are teaching the Stay.

- Put your puppy in a Sit or a Down, and use a hand signal (flat palm, facing the dog) to show that he is to stay in position. Step a pace away from the dog. Wait a second, step back and reward him. If you have a lively pup, you may find it easier to train this exercise on the lead.
- Repeat the exercise, gradually increasing the distance you can leave your dog. When you return to your dog's side, praise him quietly, and release him with a command, such as "OK".

- Remember to keep your body language very still when you are training this exercise, and avoid eye contact with your dog. Work on this exercise over a period of time, and you will build up a really reliable Stay.

SOCIALISATION

While your Bull Terrier is mastering basic obedience exercises, there is other, equally important, work to do with him. A Bull Terrier is not only becoming a part of your home and family, he is becoming a member of the community. He needs to be able to live in the outside world, coping calmly with every new situation that comes his way. It is your job to introduce him to as many different experiences as possible, and encourage him to behave in an appropriate manner.

In order to socialise your Bull Terrier effectively, it is helpful to understand how his brain is developing, and then you will get a perspective on how he sees the world.

CANINE SOCIALISATION
(Birth to 7 weeks)

This is the time when a dog learns how to be a dog. By interacting with his mother and his littermates, a young pup

Early socialisation comes from puppies interacting with their mother and with each other. *Alice van Kempen.*

learns about leadership and submission. He learns to read body posture so that he understands the intentions of his mother and his siblings. A puppy that is taken away from his litter too early may always have behavioural problems with other dogs, either being fearful or aggressive.

SOCIALISATION PERIOD
(7 to 12 weeks)
This is the time to get cracking and introduce your Bully puppy to as many different experiences as possible. This includes meeting different people, other dogs and animals, seeing new sights, and hearing a range of

sounds, from the vacuum cleaner to the roar of traffic. At this stage, a puppy learns very quickly and what he learns will stay with him for the rest of his life. This is the best time for a puppy to move to a new home, as he is adaptable and ready to form deep bonds.

FEAR-IMPRINT PERIOD
(8 to 11 weeks)
This occurs during the socialisation period, and it can be the cause of problems if it is not handled carefully. If a pup is exposed to a frightening or painful experience, it will lead to lasting impressions. Obviously, you will attempt to avoid frightening situations, but you

cannot always protect your puppy from the unexpected. If your pup has a nasty experience – such as being frightened by a motorbike zooming up behind him – the best plan is to make light of it and distract him by offering him a treat or a game. The pup will take the lead from you and will be reassured that there is nothing to worry about. If you mollycoddle him and sympathise with him, he is far more likely to retain the memory of his fear.

SENIORITY PERIOD
(12 to 16 weeks)
During this period, your Bull Terrier puppy starts to cut the

apron strings and becomes more independent. He will test out his status to find out who is the pack leader: him or you. Bad habits, such as play biting, which may have been seen as endearing a few weeks earlier, should be firmly discouraged. Remember to use positive, reward-based training, but make sure your puppy knows that you are the leader and must be respected.

SECOND FEAR-IMPRINT PERIOD (6 to 14 months)

This period is not as critical as the first fear-imprint period, but it should still be handled carefully. During this time your Bull Terrier may appear apprehensive, or he may show fear of something familiar. You may feel as if you have taken a backwards step, but if you adopt a calm, positive manner, your Bully will see that there is nothing to be alarmed about. Do not make your dog confront the thing that frightens him. Simply distract his attention, and give him something else to think about, such as obeying a simple command, such as "Sit" or "Down". This will give you the opportunity to praise and reward your dog, and will help to boost his confidence.

YOUNG ADULTHOOD AND MATURITY (1 to 4 years)

The timing of this phase depends on the size of the dog: the bigger the dog, the later it is. This period coincides with a dog's increased size and strength, mental as well as physical. Some

A well-socialised Bull Terrier will take all situations in his stride.

dogs, particularly those with a dominant nature, will test your leadership again and may become aggressive towards other dogs. Firmness and continued training are essential at this time so that your Bull Terrier accepts his status in the family pack.

IDEAS FOR SOCIALISATION

When you are socialising your Bull Terrier, you want him to experience as many different situations as possible. Try out some of the following ideas, which will ensure your Bully has an all-round education.

If you are taking on a rescued dog and have little knowledge of his background, it is important to work through a programme of socialisation. A young puppy soaks up new experiences like a sponge, but an older dog can still

learn. If a rescued dog shows fear or apprehension, treat him in exactly the same way as you would treat a youngster who is going through the second fear-imprint period (see earlier).

- Accustom your puppy to household noises, such as the vacuum cleaner, the television and the washing machine.
- Ask visitors to come to the door, wearing different types of clothing – for example, wearing a hat, a long raincoat, or carrying a stick or an umbrella.
- If you do not have children at home, make sure your Bully has a chance to meet and play with them. Go to a local park and watch children in the play area. You will not be able to take your Bull Terrier inside the play area, but he will see

children playing and will get used to their shouts of excitement.

- Attend puppy classes. These are designed for puppies between the ages of 12 to 20 weeks, and give pups a chance to play and interact together in a controlled, supervised environment. Your vet will have details of a local class.
- Take a walk around some quiet streets, such as a residential area, so your Bull Terrier can get used to the sound of traffic. As he becomes more confident, progress to busier areas.
- Go to a railway station. You don't have to get on a train if you don't need to, but your Bull Terrier will have the chance to experience trains, people wheeling luggage, loudspeaker announcements, and going up and down stairs and over railway bridges.
- If you live in the town, plan a trip to the country. You can enjoy a day out and provide an opportunity for your Bull Terrier to see livestock, such as

As your Bully matures, he may start to question your leadership.
Alice van Kempen.

sheep, cattle and horses.
- One of the best places for socialising a dog is at a country fair. There will be crowds of people, livestock in pens, tractors, bouncy castles, fairground rides and food stalls.

TRAINING CLUBS

Ideally, you should take your Bull Terrier to puppy classes, and then graduate to adult classes when he is older. There are lots of training clubs to choose from, but it is vital that you find a club that

provides a suitable environment for training Bull Terriers.

In the first instance, you can enquire at your veterinary practice for details of clubs in your area, or you can ask friends who have dogs if they attend a club. Alternatively, use the internet to find out more information. But before you take your Bull Terrier to a training club, ask if you can go to a class as an observer and find out the following:

- What experience does the instructor(s) have?
- Do they have experience with Bull Terriers? This is very important; the Bull Terrier was originally bred as a fighting dog, and if he is put into a stressful situation, this instinct may well come to the fore.
- Is the class well organised, and are the dogs reasonably quiet? (A noisy class indicates an unruly atmosphere, which will not be conducive to learning.)
- Are there are a number of classes to suit dogs of different ages and abilities?
- Are positive, reward-based training methods used?
- Does the club train for the

Good Citizen Scheme (see page 101).

If you are not happy with the training club, find another one. An inexperienced instructor who cannot handle a number of dogs in a confined environment can do more harm than good.

THE ADOLESCENT BULL TERRIER

It happens to every dog – and every owner. One minute you have a youngster who is behaving well and is happy to co-operate, and the next you have a boisterous adolescent who appears to have forgotten everything he learnt. This applies equally to males and females, although the type of adolescent behaviour, and its onset, varies between individuals.

In most cases, a Bull Terrier male will hit adolescence at around seven months, and you would not expect a dog to be fully mature until he is two years old. Generally, a male Bull Terrier will not change dramatically in personality during this time, but he will certainly test the boundaries. He will be his usual loving self, but he will test you to see if you are on your mettle. Female Bull Terriers show adolescent behaviour as they approach their first season, which is generally between six and nine months. At this time, a female Bull Terrier may become a little moody and hormonal. It is not unlike a woman suffering from PMT.

In reality, adolescence is not

Exuberant behaviour is part of the breed's charm, but it needs to be curbed otherwise your Bully will start to rule the roost. *Alice van Kempen*

the nightmare period you may imagine, if you see it from your Bull Terrier's perspective. Just like a teenager, an adolescent male Bully feels the need to flex his muscles and challenge the status quo. He may become disobedient and break house rules as he tests your authority and your role as leader. A female is generally less challenging in her behaviour. She is unlikely to thwart your authority directly, but she may be scheming and manipulative to see if she can get her own way. In both cases, your response must be firm, fair and consistent. If you show that you are a strong leader (see page 80) and are

quick to reward good behaviour, your Bull Terrier will accept you as his protector and provider.

WHEN THINGS GO WRONG

Positive, reward-based training has proved to be the most effective method of teaching dogs, but what happens when your Bull Terrier does something wrong and you need to show him that his behaviour is unacceptable? The old-fashioned school of dog training used to rely on the powers of punishment and negative reinforcement. A dog who raided the bin, for example, was smacked. Now we have learnt that it is not only unpleasant and cruel to hit a dog, it is also ineffective. If you hit a dog for stealing, he is more than likely to see you as the bad consequence of stealing, so he may raid the bin again, but probably not when you are around. If he raided the bin some time before you discovered it, he will be even more confused by your punishment, as he will not relate your response to his 'crime'. It is important to remember that unless you catch your Bull Terrier red-handed, he will not understand what he is being punished for.

There are a number of strategies to tackle undesirable behaviour – and they have nothing to do with harsh handling.

Ignoring bad behaviour: A lot of undesirable behaviour in young Bull Terriers is to do with over-exuberance. This trait is part of the breed's charm, but it can lead to difficult and sometimes dangerous situations. For example, a young Bull Terrier that repeatedly jumps up at visitors will eventually knock someone over unless he is stopped. In this case, the Bully is seeking attention, and so the best plan is to ignore him. Do not look at him, do not speak to him, and do not push him down – all

these actions are rewarding for your Bull Terrier. But someone who turns their back on him and offers no response is plain boring. The moment your Bull Terrier has four feet on the ground, give him lots of praise and maybe a treat.

If you repeat this often enough, the Bull Terrier will learn that jumping up does not have any good consequences, such as getting attention. Instead he is ignored. However, when he has all four feet on the ground, he gets loads of attention. He links the action with the consequence, and chooses the action that is most rewarding. You will find that this strategy works well with all attention-seeking behaviour, such as barking, whining or scrabbling at doors. Being ignored is a worst-case scenario for a Bull Terrier, so remember to use it as an effective training tool.

Stopping bad behaviour: There are occasions when you want to call an instant halt to whatever it is your Bull Terrier is doing. He may have just jumped on the sofa, or you may have caught him red-handed in the rubbish bin. He has already committed the 'crime', so your aim is to stop him and to redirect his attention. You can do this by using a deep, firm tone of voice to say "No", which will startle him, and then call him to you in a bright, happy voice. If necessary, you can attract him with a toy or a treat. The moment your Bull Terrier stops the undesirable behaviour and comes towards you, you can reward his good behaviour. You

There are moments when you catch your Bull Terrier red-handed, and you need to call an instant halt to his behaviour.

can back this up by running through a couple of simple exercises, such as a Sit or a Down, and rewarding with treats. In this way, your Bull Terrier focuses his attention on you, and sees you as the greatest source of reward and pleasure. Bear in mind that the Bully is a stubborn character, and it may take him longer to get the message than other breeds.

In a more extreme situation, when you want to interrupt undesirable behaviour, and you know that a simple "No" will not do the trick, you can try something a little more dramatic. If you get a can and fill it with pebbles, it will make a really loud noise when you shake it or throw it. The same effect can be achieved with purpose-made training discs, or by directing a jet of water from a water pistol at your Bully. The dog will be startled and stop what he is doing. Even better, the dog will not associate the unpleasant noise with you. This gives you the perfect opportunity to be the nice guy, calling the dog to you and giving him lots of praise.

PROBLEM BEHAVIOUR

If you have trained your Bull Terrier from puppyhood, survived his adolescence and established yourself as a fair and consistent leader, you will end up with a brilliant companion dog. The Bull Terrier is a well-balanced dog who is easy to live with – as long as you provide an environment where he knows where he stands.

However, problems may arise

unexpectedly, or you may have taken on a rescued Bull Terrier that has established behavioural problems. If you are worried about your Bull Terrier and feel out of your depth, do not delay in seeking professional help. This is readily available, usually through a referral from your vet, or you can find out additional information on the internet (see Appendices for web addresses). An animal behaviourist will have experience in tackling problem behaviour and will be able to help both you and your dog.

DOMINANCE

If you have trained and socialised

your Bull Terrier correctly, he will know his place in the family pack and will have no desire to challenge your authority. If you think of your Bully as a two-and-a-half-year-old child in a dog suit, you will not go far wrong! A toddler needs guidance to understand what is considered acceptable and unacceptable behaviour, and a Bull Terrier is exactly the same. Both dog and child need a figure in their lives that they can respect so that the daunting task of decision-making is taken from them. A Bull Terrier does not want to be the boss; in fact, a Bull Terrier that is forced into this situation will often be

Despite your best intentions, you may find yourself having to cope with undesirable behaviour. *Alice van Kempen.*

very stressed and will become deviant in his behaviour simply because he cannot cope with the situation he is faced with.

Dominance is expressed in many different ways, which may include the following:

- Showing lack of respect for your personal space. For example, your dog will barge through doors ahead of you or jump up at you.
- Getting up on to the sofa or your favourite armchair, and growling when you tell him to get back on the floor.
- Becoming possessive over a toy, or guarding his food bowl by growling when you get too close.
- Growling when anyone approaches his bed or gets too close to where he is lying.
- Ignoring basic obedience commands.
- Showing no respect to younger members of the family, pushing amongst them and completely ignoring them.
- Male dogs may start marking (cocking their leg) in the house.
- Aggression towards people, which is completely unacceptable in a Bull Terrier (see page 100).

If you see signs of your Bull Terrier becoming dominant, you must work at lowering his status

Do not be confrontational with your Bully or he will simply dig in his heels and refuse to co-operate.

so that he realises that you are the leader and he must accept your authority. Although you need to be firm, you also need to use positive training methods so that your Bull Terrier is rewarded for the behaviour you want. In this way, his 'correct' behaviour will be strengthened and repeated.

There are a number of steps you can take to lower your Bull Terrier's status. They include:

- Go back to basics and work at basic training exercises. Make sure you have some really tasty treats, or find a toy that your Bull Terrier really values and only bring it out at training sessions. Run through all the training exercises you have taught your Bull Terrier. Make a big fuss of him and reward him when he does well. This will reinforce the message that you are the leader and that it is rewarding to do as you ask.
- Avoid confrontations. If your Bull Terrier is refusing to move from the sofa, for example, do not stand over him, staring him in the eye and demanding he moves. A Bull Terrier will simply dig in his heels and refuse to budge. You will end up the loser and will have lost status in your Bull Terrier's eyes. The best plan is to offer him a toy or a treat – or even his food bowl – so that he comes to you willingly. Praise him and give him the reward you have offered. In this way, your Bully learns that co-operation is more rewarding than having his own way.
- Teach your Bull Terrier something new; this can be as simple as learning a trick, such

as shaking paws. Having something new to think about will mentally stimulate your Bull Terrier and he will benefit from interacting with you.

- Be 100 per cent consistent with all house rules – your Bull Terrier must never sit on the sofa, and you must never allow him to jump up at you.
- If your Bull Terrier has been guarding his food bowl, put the bowl down empty and drop in a little food at a time. Periodically stop dropping in the food, and tell your Bully to "Sit" and "Wait". Give it a few seconds, and then reward him by dropping in more food. This shows your Bull Terrier that you are the provider of the food, and he can only eat when you allow him to.
- Make sure the family eats before you feed your Bull Terrier. Some trainers advocate eating in front of the dog (maybe just a few bites from a biscuit) before starting a training session, so the dog appreciates your elevated status.
- Do not let your Bull Terrier barge through doors ahead of you, or leap from the back of

There is evidence that there is an inherited link to obsessive behaviour. *Alice van Kempen.*

the car before you release him. You may need to put your dog on the lead and teach him to "Wait" at doorways, and then reward him for letting you go through first.

If you work hard with his retraining programme, your Bull Terrier will come to realise that you are the decision-maker and he will not seek to challenge your authority. In most cases, a Bull Terrier will be relieved when he has found his 'correct' place in the family pack. However, if your Bull Terrier is still trying to be dominant, or you have any other concerns, do not delay in seeking the help of an animal behaviourist.

TIME OUT

The Bull Terrier is generally a laid-back character, and if he is brought up to accept short periods of separation from his owner, there is no reason why he should become anxious. A new puppy should be left for short periods on his own, ideally in a crate where he cannot get up to any mischief. It is a good idea to leave him with a boredom-busting toy (see page 51) so he will be happily occupied in your absence. When you return, do not rush to the crate and make a huge fuss. Wait a few minutes, and then calmly go to the crate and release your dog, telling him how good he has been. If this scenario is repeated a number of times, your Bull Terrier will soon learn that being left on his own is no big deal.

OBSESSIVE BEHAVIOUR

The Bull Terrier is a single-minded dog; once he becomes focused, it is very hard to change his mindset. It may seem funny when a Bull Terrier puppy chases his tail, repeatedly runs after a tennis ball, tries to chase the vacuum cleaner, or grabs a broom – but if you see signs of this type of behaviour, it needs to be halted straight away.

A Bull Terrier has a tendency to

become obsessive in his behaviour, and something that started as a game can become full-blown compulsive behaviour. There are stories of Bull Terriers whose lives – and their owners' lives – have become a misery because of obsessive behaviour. A Bull Terrier is so focused, and so determined, he will chase and bite his tail until it bleeds, or spend every waking minute in search of a tennis ball.

There is now evidence that obsessive/compulsive behaviour is an inherited problem in Bull Terriers. There is a researcher in America working on this and reports have been published. Obviously, how badly a Bull Terrier that is only mildly afflicted displays these characteristics depends on his environment. If you lock him in a kennel for 23 hours a day and pay him no

attention, these traits will come to the fore if they are genetically present. A low level of OCB could manifest as a fixation on, for example, a ball. Occasional tail chasing is a higher level; compulsive tail chasing and chewing on feet etc are the serious results.

As in so many cases, prevention is better than cure. Do not let your Bull Terrier puppy chase his tail, run after a ball, or chase the vacuum cleaner. You can distract his behaviour by offering him a treat, or maybe producing a toy and inviting him to play with you. If your Bully seems determined, try putting him in his crate or out in the garden when you are vacuuming or sweeping. Remember, the more opportunities a Bull Terrier has to repeat a behaviour, the more likely it is to become a habit.

AGGRESSION

Aggression is a complex issue, as there are different causes and the behaviour may be triggered by numerous factors. In the case of a Bull Terrier, it very rarely directed towards people, but far more commonly it is directed towards other dogs. Aggression in dogs may be the result of:

- Dominance (see page 97).
- Territory: A dog may become aggressive if strange dogs or people enter his territory (which is generally seen as the house and garden).
- Intra-sexual issues: This is aggression between male-to-male or female-to-female.
- Parental instinct: A mother dog may become aggressive if she is protecting her puppies.
- Defensive behaviour: This may be induced by fear, pain or punishment.

Do not allow your Bull Terrier to get involved in situations that might escalate out of control. *Alice van Kempen.*

As we have discussed, the old Bull-and-Terriers were bred as fighting dogs, and owners need to be aware of this aspect of their dog's origins. In the case of a Bully, his attitude seems to be that, if threatened or challenged, he will get the first punch in. If he is exposed to this sort of situation at an early age, he may well adopt this approach when he meets other dogs. He does not wait to be attacked – he gets in there first.

The best approach is to socialise your Bull Terrier with dogs of impeccable temperament so that his inbred response is diluted. If he is not challenged, his instinct to protect himself will not be fired. Ideally, this process of socialisation should start from puppyhood and then be an on-going process throughout your dog's life. The golden rule is not to put your Bull Terrier in a situation that could prove hazardous – it is your job to have control of your Bully at all times.

If you have taken on an older, rescued dog, you will have little or no knowledge of his background, and if he shows signs of aggression, the cause will need to be determined. In most cases, you would be well advised to call in professional help if you see aggressive behaviour in your dog in situations that you cannot manage. This type of behaviour can escalate very quickly and could lead to disastrous consequences.

NEW CHALLENGES
If you enjoy training your Bull Terrier, you may want to try one

The aim is to have a well-behaved Bull Terrier that can be part of the family activities. *Alice van Kempen.*

of the many dog sports that are now on offer. Training a Bull Terrier will certainly be a challenge – but if you make it fun, your Bull Terrier will enter into the spirit of it, and will enjoy spending quality time with you.

GOOD CITIZEN SCHEME
This is a scheme run by the Kennel Club in the UK and the American Kennel Club in the USA. The schemes promote responsible ownership and help you to train a well-behaved dog who will fit in with the community. The schemes are excellent for all pet owners, and are certainly within a Bull Terrier's compass. The KC and the AKC schemes vary in format. In the UK there are three levels: bronze, silver and gold, with each test becoming progressively more demanding. In the AKC scheme there is a single test.

Some of the exercises include:
• Walking on a loose lead among people and other dogs.
• Recall amid distractions.

• A controlled greeting where dogs stay under control while owners meet.
• The dog allows all-over grooming and handling by his owner, and also accepts being handled by the examiner.
• Stays, with the owner in sight, and then out of sight.
• Food manners, allowing the owner to eat without begging, and taking a treat on command.
• Sendaway – sending the dog to his bed.

The tests are designed to show the control you have over your dog, and his ability to respond correctly and remain calm in all situations. The Good Citizen Scheme is taught at most training clubs. For more information, log on to the Kennel Club or AKC website (see Appendices).

SHOWING
In your eyes, your Bull Terrier is the most beautiful dog in the

world – but would a judge agree? Showing is a highly competitive sport and breeding a top-quality Bull Terrier is a highly skilled business. However, many owners get bitten by the showing bug, and their calendar is governed by the dates of the top showing fixtures.

To be successful in the show ring, a Bull Terrier must conform as closely as possible to the Breed Standard, a written blueprint describing the 'perfect' Bull Terrier (see Chapter Seven). To get started you need to buy a puppy that has show potential and then train him to perform in the ring. A Bull Terrier will be expected to stand in show pose, gait for the judge in order to show off his natural movement, and to be examined by the judge. This involves a detailed hands-on examination, so your Bull Terrier must be bombproof when handled by strangers.

Many training clubs hold ringcraft classes, which are run by experienced showgoers. At these classes, you will learn how to handle your Bull Terrier in the ring, and you will also find out about rules, procedures and show-ring etiquette.

The best plan is to start off at some small, informal shows where you can practise and learn the tricks of the trade before graduating to bigger shows. It's a long haul starting in the very first

Showing is highly competitive at the top level.

puppy class, but the dream is to make your Bull Terrier up into a Champion.

COMPETITIVE OBEDIENCE
Border Collies and German Shepherds dominate this sport in the UK, but in the USA there is more widespread interest in competing with different breeds. The Bull Terrier is more of the officer class than the infantry, and he does not thrive on drilling and repetition. He is a dog who likes to think for himself, and unless you can make obedience fun, he will not see the point of it.

However, for those owners who like a challenge, you will need to train the following exercises:

- **Heelwork:** Dog and handler must complete a set pattern on and off the lead, which

includes left turns, right turns, about turns, and changes of pace.
- **Recall:** This may be when the handler is stationary or on the move.
- **Retrieve:** This may be a dumbbell or any article chosen by the judge.
- **Sendaway:** The dog is sent to a designated spot and must go into an instant Down until he is recalled by the handler.
- **Stays:** The dog must stay in the Sit and in the Down for a set amount of time. In advanced classes, the handler is out of sight.
- **Scent:** The dog must retrieve a single cloth from a pre-arranged pattern of cloths that has his owner's scent, or, in advanced classes, the judge's scent. There may also be decoy cloths.
- **Distance control.** The dog must execute a series of moves (Sit, Stand, Down) without moving from his position and with the handler at a distance.

Even though competitive obedience requires accuracy and precision, ensure you make it fun for your Bull Terrier, with lots of praise and rewards so that you motivate him to do his best. Many training clubs run advanced classes for those who want to compete in obedience, or you can hire the services of a professional trainer so you can have one-on-one sessions.

If you put in the work training and socialising your Bull Terrier you will be rewarded with an outstanding companion.
Alice van Kempen.

AGILITY

This fun sport has grown enormously in popularity over the past few years. If you fancy having a go, make sure you have good control over your Bull Terrier and keep him slim. Agility is a very physical sport, which demands fitness from both dog and handler. A fat dog is never going to make it as a serious contender in agility competitons.

In agility competitions, each dog must complete a set course over a series of obstacles, which include:

- Jumps (upright hurdles and long jump)
- Weaves
- A-frame
- Dog walk
- Seesaw
- Tunnels (collapsible and rigid)
- Tyre

Dogs may compete in jumping classes with jumps, tunnels and weaves, or in agility classes, which have the full set of equipment. Faults are awarded for poles down on the jumps, missed contact points on the A-frame, dog walk and seesaw, and refusals. If a dog takes the wrong course, he is eliminated. The winner is the dog that completes the course in the fastest time with no faults. As you progress up the levels, courses become progressively harder with more twists, turns and changes of direction.

If you want to get involved in agility, you will need to find a club that specialises in the sport (see Appendices).

You will not be allowed to start training until your Bull Terrier is 12 months old, and you cannot compete until he is 18 months old. This rule is for the protection of the dog, who may suffer injury if he puts strain on bones and joints while he is still growing.

SUMMING UP

The Bull Terrier is a breed that has its own very special charm. He adores his family, but is not too clingy; he has a strong character but will accept your leadership; and he has a unique sense of humour. Although you are unlikely to train a top obedience Champion, with a little work and a lot of commonsense, you can produce a companion dog that is second to none.

CASE HISTORY

Author Jane Killion lives with a house full of Bull Terriers and a very wise cat in Blairstown, New Jersey. She breeds and shows Bull Terriers and has competed successfully in agility and obedience with them.

You can find out more about her methods by reading her highly-acclaimed book *When Pigs Fly! Training Success With Impossible Dogs* (see page 147).

Who says a Bully can't be trained? Jane working with Ruby.

' My family brought home our first Bull Terrier 26 years ago. From the moment that little white piglet walked into the house, there was no turning back – we fell head over heels in love with the breed. The Bull Terrier's profoundly affectionate nature is the single quality that most attracts me. He combines steely determination, intense joie de vivre, and a heart of gold into one fine-looking package. Bullies are devoted to their families and have a great sense of propriety and harmony, yet they are not keen on following externally imposed rules. That corresponds with my outlook on life, so Bull Terriers are a great match for me.

I love my dogs, and I love doing active and competitive things, so it was natural for me to get involved with my dogs in every discipline available to us. I first got involved in agility ten years ago. I took one of my youngsters to a training class that included agility equipment. I saw how quickly she picked up on the behaviours, and how joyful she was when actually doing agility. I also discovered how hard it was to keep her from running away as far as she could, as fast as she could, the second the leash came off. It was that paradox of talent and extreme indifference to training that intrigued me and I was determined to find a way to get through to this animal.

I knew there was a key to unlocking the potential in my dog, and I did eventually find it – not before spending a year or two chasing after and tackling her, but I did succeed in the end. So far, I have put 18 performance titles on five different Bull Terriers and I look forward to many more happy years running with my best friends.

What I discovered is that Bull Terriers are not necessarily harder or easier to train than other dogs, but they are different. They are great problem solvers and extremely persistent. They generally have very little fear and rarely suffer from shyness issues. So long as you use training methods that tap into these great qualities, rather

Zulu showing focus and precision.

Ruby negotiating the weaves.

than training methods that rely on biddability or imposition of your will, they are easy to work with.

Bull Terriers are smart and quick to learn if you appeal to their formidable problem solving abilities rather than issuing edicts. Their stubby bodies will never whip through the weave poles as quickly as a Border Collie, and their body mass means they will not perform well in heat, but, taking all in all, a Bull Terrier is a perfectly serviceable performance companion.

Are you are fortunate (or crazy) enough to own or breed show dogs? If you are, I believe you should strongly consider doing some kind of performance with your breed dogs. Taking our show dogs out in performance keeps us honest and proves our breeding programmes. Unsound dogs, dogs with unstable temperaments, or dogs of a size and bulk as to be unable to move in a performance venue are not the dogs described by the Breed Standard. On the other hand, a sound dog that does not possess virtues of head and type sufficient to become a Champion does not optimally represent the Standard, either. Speaking as a fancier and, I hope, custodian of the breed, I think that dogs titled in both performance and conformation are important contributors to keeping our breed grounded in our Standard yet moving it forward.

If you love the breed, there is no substitute for doing performance sports with your Bull Terrier. While some of the 'traditional' breeds may take their jobs more seriously and discharge those jobs with more precision, Bull Terriers shine with joy when performing, a joy that is witty and infectious, a joy that says, "Can you *believe* how fun this is?" and you can't help but feel that joy, too. My advice to you, if you want to get involved in performance sports with your Bull Terrier, is to ignore anyone who tells you it can't be done or that your dog is not interested in learning (and almost everyone will tell you this). Instead, find yourself a trainer who understands your dog or, failing that, buy every book and DVD out there on shaping behaviour and keep learning. Expect to be humiliated, expect to spend months training what others seem to be able to train in minutes, but also expect the sublime experience of everything paying off one day. If you keep trying and learning, you will eventually enjoy the indescribable pleasure of being a team with the dog you love, and nothing can top that. **,**

THE PERFECT BULL TERRIER

First and foremost, the Bull Terrier is a 'head' breed.

What is the essence of the Bull Terrier? What are those characteristics that differentiate the Bull Terrier from the hundreds of other recognised breeds? Certainly the typical Bull Terrier possesses the following traits:

- That unique Bull Terrier head and diabolical expression; in other words, it is a 'head' breed.
- Ample bone, musculature and substance; oft-times described as the maximum substance for the size, without loss of quality.
- Balance, shapeliness and symmetry – a blend of Bulldog and terrier.
- Soundness, including free, jaunty movement.
- A friendly, outgoing and fun-loving disposition – the cavalier and clown of the canine race.

It is these characteristics that are detailed in the standard of perfection for the breed, thus defining the 'perfect' Bull Terrier. A Breed Standard is a description of the perfect specimen of the breed, and it is against this ideal that dogs are judged at shows. It is important to note that we judge dogs not against each other, but rather each against their Standard, the winner being the specimen that comes closest to that description. We employ the adjectives 'ideal' and 'perfect', but in fact there is no such thing. The perfect Bull Terrier or the perfect specimen of any breed is yet to be born. The great allure of breeding and showing dogs is the goal of realising the unattainable – a specimen that exudes the essence of the breed, meeting the requirements of the Standard

107

A top-class British Bull Terrier: Villensia Snowblind at Bullyview.

completely in every respect. We are seeking virtues rather than lack of faults. Top breeders talk about blameless nonentities – dogs that eschew faults but equally lack outstanding virtues. Of course, most pet owners believe their own Bull Terrier is simply the best; he may be a wonderful companion, but he may well not be a very good specimen of the breed.

THE SHOW WORLD

In the world of showing and breeding pedigree dogs, there are three principal governing bodies that have written and officially approved the Breed Standards: the Kennel Club (KC) in the United Kingdom, the Federation Cynologique Internationale (FCI), and the American Kennel Club (AKC). The KC and AKC are both national organisations, whereas the FCI, based in Belgium, provides Standards and show regulations for some 83 member countries:

- Continental European countries (33 countries)
- South America (Argentina, Brazil, Ecuador, Colombia, Chile, Mexico, Panama, Puerto Rico, Dominican Republic, Uruguay and Venezuela)
- Israel, Morocco, South Korea, Japan, Philippines and Thailand
- A number of other countries

are associated, but not affiliated, with the FCI. They include Australia, Ireland and South Africa.

These three governing bodies classify pedigree dogs into different groups, depending on the breed's background and working ancestry. Each body includes the Bull Terrier as a member of the Terrier Group. It is usual for a breed's country of origin to have a dominant influence on the Standard for that breed around the world. With the Bull Terrier having been developed in England, naturally the UK Standard has led the way, with other Standards simply

Am. Ch. Magor Margo of Misk: A top winner in North America.

A show winner under FCI rules. *Alice van Kempen.*

offering minor variations on this theme. Over the past few decades, however, the Bull Terrier's Standards defined by the KC, FCI and AKC have drifted a little further apart, primarily due to recent changes made to the KC Standard not being reflected in the other Standards. The KC version was last updated in September 2007, the FCI's in 1987, while the AKC's has remained unchanged since 1974, a Standard which itself is not significantly different from the 1957 version. These recent changes in the UK are not substantial; indeed, many aficionados of the breed would argue that they were unnecessary.

Nonetheless, they have further distanced the Standards in terms of format and precise wording. On the other hand, an exceptionally fine Bull Terrier would be judged as such whichever Standard is applied, as would a very poor specimen.

THE BULL TERRIER STANDARDS OF PERFECTION

The wording of the Breed Standard paints a vision of the perfect Bull Terrier and it is this visualisation that conformation show judges use as the basis of their assessment of the dogs. But it is very rare for two people to

interpret the Standard in precisely the same way. One judge may view a certain fault very harshly and eliminate an exhibit with this fault from further consideration, awarding first place to an exhibit that, in other respects, is less worthy. Because of these differing perspectives on faults and virtues, a wonderfully 'typy' Bull Terrier – typy here referring to the virtues essential to breed perfection – may be beaten by a specimen of apparently lesser type. In the world of Bull Terriers, there is a strong preference towards breeder-judges – in other words, judges who also breed Bullies. Such judges are likely to be more forgiving of faults and to focus on

JUDGING THE BULL TERRIER

It is the judge's job to interpret the Breed Standard and find the dog that comes closest to the 'ideal'. Every dog will be given a thorough 'hands on' examination.

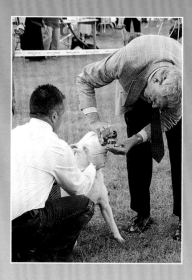

The Bull Terrier is a strongly built, muscular dog but should appear balanced and active. *Alice van Kempen.*

virtues. On the other hand, all-rounders – judges who are qualified to adjudicate many breeds and have no particular association with Bullies – are viewed, rightly or wrongly, as prone to penalising faults at the expense of virtues.

We have learned that the Bull Terrier was developed by combining other breeds. Fanciers talk about specimens that are more 'bully' in type or more 'terrierish'. The 'bully' type tends to excel in bone and substance and may be slightly lower to the ground. The 'terrier' type is lighter in bone, compact and exudes quality and agility. Fanciers also refer to a third variation, which some call 'houndy', others the 'Dalmatian' type. These tend to be well up on the leg, excelling in shapeliness and freedom of movement. None of these variations is ideal. The perfect Bull Terrier, as portrayed in the Standard, takes the middle ground, combining the virtues of each while discarding those features that stray from the essence of the breed.

DETAILED ANALYSIS

In this section we review and compare the current UK, FCI and AKC Standards. As mentioned above, they differ in both format and detail, which necessitates grouping some of the sections. In America, and only in America, the Bull Terrier is separated into two varieties – White and Colored – with a Standard for each. Fortunately, the one for the Colored Variety states that it 'is the same as for the White except for the sub head 'Color'.'

Responding to public concern about the health of pure bred dogs, the KC has inserted the following introductory paragraph in all breed Standards:

A Breed Standard is the guideline which describes the ideal characteristics, temperament and appearance of a breed and ensures that the breed is fit for function. Absolute soundness is essential. Breeders and judges should at all times be careful to avoid obvious conditions or exaggerations which would be detrimental in any way to the health, welfare or soundness of this breed. From time to time certain conditions or exaggerations may be considered to have the potential to affect dogs in some breeds adversely, and judges and breeders are requested to refer to the Kennel Club website for details of any such current issues. If a feature or quality is desirable it should only be present in the right measure.

GENERAL APPEARANCE, CHARACTERISTICS AND TEMPERAMENT

KC
General Appearance: Strongly built, muscular, well balanced and active with a keen, determined and intelligent

expression. Characteristics: Courageous, full of spirit, with a fun loving attitude. A unique feature is a downfaced, egg-shaped head. Irrespective of size dogs should look masculine and bitches feminine. Temperament: Of even temperament and amenable to discipline. Although obstinate, is particularly good with people.

AKC
The Bull Terrier must be strongly built, muscular, symmetrical and active, with a keen determined and intelligent expression, full of fire but of sweet disposition and amenable to discipline.

FCI
General Appearance: Strongly built, muscular, well balanced

and active with a keen, determined and intelligent expression. A unique feature is a downfaced, eggshaped head. Irrespective of size dogs should look masculine and bitches feminine. Behaviour and Temperament: The Bull Terrier is the gladiator of the canine race, full of fire and courageous. Of even temperament and amenable to discipline. Although obstinate is particularly good with people.

These sections of the Standards provide us with a framework on which to build our image of the ideal specimen, with the details to follow. The KC narrative covers most of the key characteristics well: strong build, yet balanced and active; keen expression and egg-shaped head; spirited and fun-loving; dogs look masculine, bitches feminine; good with people, obstinate but amenable to discipline. The FCI version is close, but retains the older wording, describing the Bully as the gladiator of the canine world, an unfortunate expression in a time of breed-specific legislation and anti-dog sentiment. The phrase was introduced into the KC Standard in 1915; it was descriptive in the sense that Bull Terriers are supposed to appear muscular and athletic, but they were never intended as fighting dogs, which 'gladiator' implies. The phrase was dropped only recently in the UK. Providentially, it was never adopted in America.

The AKC provides a briefer introductory paragraph, preferring to review head and expression in later sections. Also there is no mention of dogs appearing masculine and bitches feminine anywhere in the AKC Standard. Yet the sex of a Bully should be apparent at a glance, without having to check the nether parts, so the omission is not a desirable one.

We could criticise the KC version for separating "Courageous, full of spirit with a fun loving attitude" from 'Temperament'. "Of even temperament" doesn't do justice to the breed. Better to say, "courageous, fun loving, spirited, at times obstinate, yet amenable to discipline," which speaks of their captivating, multi-faceted personality. And, of course, they love people and especially kids. Remember: Bullies thrive when integrated into their family's life.

Clearly the Bully should offer a lot of dog in a small compass. The flip side to strong and muscular is the retention of quality, activity and free movement. The Bully is not the canine equivalent of a body builder and should never be clumsy.

And without a typical head and expression, a Bully can't be a show specimen. Their expression is variously described as 'varminty', diabolical and wicked, which, of course, belies their

The head is long and strong, with no hint of coarseness.

friendly disposition. These characteristics are reviewed under the next several headings.

HEAD AND SKULL

KC

Head and Skull: Head long, strong and deep right to end of muzzle, but not coarse. Viewed from front egg-shaped and completely filled, its surface free from hollows or indentations. Top of skull almost flat from ear to ear. Profile curves gently downwards from top of skull to tip of nose which should be black and bent downwards at

tip. Nostrils well developed and under-jaw deep and strong.

AKC

Head: Should be long, strong and deep right to the end of the muzzle, but not coarse. Full face it should be oval in outline and be filled completely up giving the impression of fullness with a surface devoid of hollows or indentations, i.e., egg shaped. In profile it should curve gently downwards from the top of the skull to the tip of the nose. The forehead should be flat across from ear to ear. The distance from the tip of the nose to the eyes should be

perceptibly greater than that from the eyes to the top of the skull. The underjaw should be deep and well defined.

FCI

Head: Long, strong and deep right to end of muzzle, but not coarse. Viewed from front eggshaped and completely filled, its surface free from hollows or indentations. Profile curves gently downwards from top of skull to tip of nose. Cranial Region: Skull: Top of skull almost flat from ear to ear.

The Bull Terrier is a head breed. Without a typical head and expression, a Bully may be a wonderful companion but just isn't typical, lacking a primary characteristic of the breed. Also a Bully with a poor head and expression has a strong tendency to perpetuate these faults when bred. But this does not mean that the head over-rides the overall dog. Judges should first assess virtues, like a superior head and expression, and then take account of faults. So a superbly headed Bully that is coarse, unsound and unbalanced overall – in other words, one that has a head and nothing else – should be penalised appropriately when being placed in a class. The same should apply to a specimen that is sound and representative behind the collar but is totally lacking in head and expression. Indeed, such a Bully is not a show specimen.

Again there are some differences among the Standards, not in essence but rather in which sections particular characteristics are discussed. The use of 'egg-shaped' tells us that the Bully head is filled and free from hollows; really, three ways of saying the same thing. Breeders talk about filled up or packed beneath the eyes; again, the same thing. Eggs are also curved in profile and each of three Standards calls for a gentle downwards curve. This feature is often described as 'downface'. Ideally, the Bully head should present an unbroken curve to the tip of the muzzle. The KC Standard also covers the nose, which should be bent downwards at the tip, whereas the AKC and FCI cover this feature under a specific section on the nose; we will follow the AKC/FCI structure.

For many decades, breeders struggled to develop the egg-shaped head with that gently curved profile. By the late 1970s/early 1980s, when these virtues were appearing consistently among the top winners, breeders began a new quest – the more dramatic the profile, the better: let's go way beyond gentle and exaggerate the profile! The Standard still says gentle, but exaggeration has become fashionable in the UK and especially in North America. These dramatic profiles are causing fundamental changes to the shape of the head, which, again, can be argued to be at odds with each Standard. The KC and AKC versions call for a strong and deep head right to the end of the muzzle and also for a deep underjaw (plus KC: strong, and AKC: well-defined). These

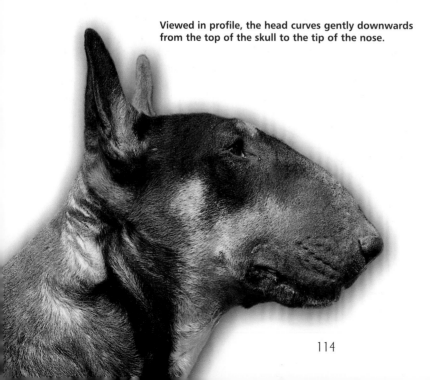

Viewed in profile, the head curves gently downwards from the top of the skull to the tip of the nose.

requirements also imply ample width of muzzle and underjaw. Dramatic profiles tend to result in a narrowing of the head. Anything approaching a parrot-shaped head is an anathema in Bullies. In addition, narrowing of the upper and lower jaws means that the teeth have less space in which to develop. We will discuss this later.

The muzzle should also be long. The AKC Standard requires the distance from the tip of the nose to the eyes to be perceptibly greater than that from the eyes to the top of the skull. Both the KC and FCI make equivalent statements under the section on eyes. Many breeds demand equal length of muzzle and skull, but the Bull Terrier is among those that must have a muzzle that is noticeably longer. Finally, the skull should be flat between the ears, which are set close together, so this distance is relatively short. The KC and FCI say "almost" flat; the AKC simply states flat.

EYES

KC and FCI

Eyes: Appearing narrow, obliquely placed and triangular, well sunken (*triangular, well sunken* recently deleted from the KC Standard), black or as dark brown as possible so as to appear almost black, and with a piercing glint. Distance from

The triangular-shaped eyes should be as dark as possible with a piercing glint. *Alice van Kempen.*

tip of nose to eyes perceptibly greater than that from eyes to top of skull. Blue or partly blue undesirable.

AKC

Eyes: Should be well sunken and as dark as possible, with a piercing glint and they should be small, triangular and obliquely placed; set near together and high up on the dog's head. Blue eyes are a disqualification.

The KC Standard used to call for the eyes to be black or as dark brown as possible. Today both the KC and FCI have dropped "black", whereas AKC simply states as dark as possible. Certainly they should be dark. Any tendency to lightness is a fault that detracts from the Bully's unique expression. Blue eyes have long been associated with

deafness and so were for many years a disqualification. The KC, however, has now replaced disqualifications with the term undesirable. So the KC and FCI say undesirable, while AKC retains the disqualification.

The KC and FCI position the "distance from tip of nose . . ." under eyes, but otherwise the Standards are very similar. The AKC version provides one extra phrase – set close together – that arguably should be included in the other standards. Thus the Bully's eyes should be small, dark, well sunken (not prominent), triangular in shape, set high/obliquely and set relatively close together. All of these factors are important. The deletion of "triangular, well sunken" from the description signals a concern that these features might lead to eye problems, for example entropion (the eye lashes turn inwards). This is a relatively rare condition in Bull Terriers and certainly not one that breeders associate with eyes that are triangular and well sunken. "Triangular", of course, refers to the shape of the opening not the eye itself. The opening is not precisely triangular, but anything approaching an oval or round opening detracts to a surprising degree from the Bully's expression. Equally "well sunken" should not be taken to mean excessively sunken, but the eyes must be set sufficiently deeply to protect them from injury.

The ears should be small, thin and placed close together.

The Standards are clear on their definition of ears – small, thin and close together. Small, close together and held stiffly erect contribute significantly to the typical Bully expression; thick and wide-set ears detract. Too often we see Bullies with ears that are larger and thicker than the ideal; too often they are set wider and flare out too much to the side. We still see a goodly range of ear shapes, sizes, thicknesses and settings in the show ring today. Often ears are too open and flat rather than being nicely sculpted. Smaller Bullies tend more towards correct ears than very large ones. So it is an infrequent delight to see a Bully with ideal ear type and carriage. Be aware that some Bullies prefer to hold their ears in a relaxed position, lying on the back of the head; however, they must be able to hold them alertly erect when called on to do so. As an aside, many Bull Terrier pups need help with getting their ears to stand erectly. Your breeder can advise on this procedure using allogenic adhesive tape

Remember, with the oval shape of the head the Bully's eyes are exposed far more than in breeds that sport a distinct stop and in which the eyes are set to look straight ahead – Staffordshire Bull Terriers for example. Clearly the Bully's eyes must be set deeply enough to protect them for injury and in no way appear prominent.

This precipitous change by the KC further distances the British standard from the older version retained in America.

Anything approaching a round opening and a prominent eye detract greatly from the Bully's expression, as does a low setting; these faults all contribute to what breeders call a common expression. Similarly light coloured eyes should be faulted according to degree. Key to the Bully's unique expression is small dark eyes set high on the skull and obliquely. Together these attributes generate that piercing glint and the impish, inscrutable, almost diabolical expression. Yet just beneath that forbidding glint we can detect the Bully's friendly and fun loving disposition.

EARS

KC and FCI
Ears: Small, thin and placed close together. Dog should be able to hold them stiffly erect, when they point straight upwards.

AKC
Ears: Should be small, thin and placed close together. They should be capable of being held stiffly erect, when they should point upwards.

LIPS, NOSE AND TEETH

KC
Mouth: Teeth sound, clean, strong, of good size, regular with perfect, regular and complete scissor bite, i.e. upper teeth closely overlapping lower teeth and set square to the jaws. Lips clean and tight.

AKC
Lips: Should be clean and tight. Teeth: Should meet in either a

level or in a scissors bite. In the scissors bite the upper teeth should fit in front of and closely against the lower teeth, and they should be sound, strong and perfectly regular. Nose: Should be black, with well-developed nostrils bent downward at the tip.

FCI

Facial Region: Nose: Should be black. Bent downwards at tip. Nostrils well developed. Lips: Clean and tight. Jaws/Teeth: Under-jaw deep and strong. Teeth sound, clean, strong, of good size, regular with a perfect, regular and complete scissor bite, i.e. upper teeth closely overlapping lower teeth and set square to the jaws.

All of the Standards agree that the lips should be clean and tight. In other words, there should be no looseness around the flews.

The AKC and FCI both deal with the nose here. It should be black with well-developed nostrils and bent downwards at the tip. This last point is a key characteristic of the Bull Terrier profile, called the Roman finish. It appears almost as if the nose had been hit and bent downwards with a hammer.

With such a powerful, muscular dog as the Bully, the teeth must be strong and of good size. For many years the requirement was for a scissors (closely overlapping) bite or a level bite (with the incisors meeting like pincers). However,

The teeth should meet in a scissor bite with the teeth on the upper jaw closely overlapping the teeth on the lower jaw.

the KC and FCI have now discarded the level bite, with only the scissors bite being correct. The AKC, on the other hand, has retained the traditional scissors or level bite. Faults occurring with Bully teeth include undershot (lower incisors project beyond upper ones) and wry bites, in-growing canine teeth and missing premolars (fewer than four on each side); overshot bites do crop up now and then.

Most judges have to face the challenge of how to assess the Bully that has incorrect dentition but is otherwise a very worthy specimen. With many breeders focussing on downface, we are progressively changing the shape of the head and often narrowing the jaws. Such changes can wreak havoc with dentition. A

more exaggerated profile reduces the effective length of the foreface; the teeth can't keep up with these changes we are generating in the bone structure and so we get undershot bites. Additionally, with narrowing jaws the teeth have less space in which to position themselves, with the result that, instead of pointing slightly outwards, the lower canines tend to develop by growing straight up into the upper jaw or even inwards into the palate. We see smaller teeth and sometimes they are not placed regularly.

So what is the judge to do? Discard any dogs with incorrect bites? As we shall see later, the seriousness of a fault should be considered in exact proportion to its degree. A reverse scissors bite, in which the lower incisors are just in front of the upper ones with no gap between them, is less serious than a totally undershot bite in which the bottom incisors and canines are well forward of the upper incisors. Are the teeth otherwise regularly spaced? Are the jaws strong and deep? The judge should penalise according to the degree of the fault and then balance each exhibit's overall virtues against its faults. To place a blameless nonentity over an exceptionally typical Bully having a minor bite problem would be an example of fault judging – the infamous blameless nonentity here being a dog that has no significant faults but, equally, fails to offer the essential virtues of the breed.

The neck is long and muscular, tapering from the shoulders to the head. The back is short and strong.

NECK

KC and FCI
Neck: Very muscular, long, arched, tapering from shoulders to head and free from loose skin.

AKC
Neck: Should be very muscular, long, arched and clean, tapering from the shoulders to the head and it should be free from loose skin.

The Standards agree upon the wording for the neck, with the AKC version adding the adjective 'clean' – implying clean lines. Note that, despite the requirement for a short back, as discussed in the next section, the Bully should have a long neck. Such a long, arched neck calls for shoulder blades of good length and well laid back; the more upright the shoulder blade, the shorter the neck. Regrettably, many Bullies sport necks that are closer to medium than long and with, consequentially, less of the proud arching that so distinguishes the correct Bully.

BODY AND CHEST

KC
Body well rounded with marked spring of rib and great depth from withers to brisket, so that latter nearer ground than belly. Back short, strong with backline behind withers level, arching or roaching slightly over broad, well muscled loins. Underline from brisket to belly forms a graceful upward curve. Chest broad when viewed from front.

AKC
Chest: Should be broad when viewed from in front, and there should be great depth from withers to brisket, so that the latter is nearer the ground than the belly. Body: Should be well rounded with marked spring of rib, the back should be short and strong. The back ribs deep. Slightly arched over the loin. The shoulders should be strong and muscular but without heaviness. The shoulder blades should be wide and flat and there should be a very

pronounced backward slope
from the bottom edge of the
blade to the top edge. Behind
the shoulders there should be
no slackness or dip at the
withers. The underline from the
brisket to the belly should form
a graceful upward curve.

FCI

Body: Well rounded with
marked spring of rib and great
depth from withers to brisket,
so that latter nearer ground
than belly. Back: Short, strong,
with backline behind withers
level, arching or roaching
slightly over loins. Loins:
Broad, well muscled.
Chest: Broad when viewed from
front. Underline: From brisket
to belly forms a graceful
upward curve.

Each version demands a short,
strong back. None of them,
however, define how short is
short. The Bully is not square like
a Fox Terrier, with the height at
the withers equalling the distance
from the forechest to the rump.
Rather, the Bully's back is slightly
longer than this, but in no way
approaching medium in length.
Too many Bull Terriers are
somewhat upright in shoulder,
which has the effect of shortening
the neck and lengthening the
back. It is surprising how often
judges are accepting of specimens
with upright shoulders, medium
length of neck and a none-too-
short back. Clearly this is not
what the Standards call for.

The ribs should be broad, deep
and well sprung – almost barrel-

like – and, although not explicitly
mentioned, they should be
carried well back to ensure a
short-coupled loin. Most judges
are accepting of a slightly longer
loin in bitches. The Bully's body
is characterised by graceful lines.
The beautifully arched neck, with
shoulders well laid back, lead to
the withers being set well along
the back; only the short middle
portion of the back is flat, as the
topline rises slightly over the
muscles of the loins. Underneath
there is that graceful upwards
curve; it should never be flat or
give any indication of a tubular

body shape. Overall the body and
limbs of the Bully can be
described as well knit and
athletic in appearance.

FOREQUARTERS AND HINDQUARTERS

KC

Forequarters: Shoulders strong
and muscular without loading.
Shoulder blades wide, flat and
held closely to chest wall and
have a very pronounced
backward slope of front edge
from bottom to top, forming
almost a right angle with upper

The Bull Terrier should stand solidly on strong, straight forelegs.

arm. Elbows held straight and strong, pasterns upright. Forelegs have strongest type of round, quality bone, dog should stand solidly upon them and they should be perfectly parallel. In mature dogs length of foreleg should be approximately equal to depth of chest. Hindquarters: Hindlegs in parallel when viewed from behind. Thighs muscular and second thighs well developed. Stifle joint well bent and hock well angulated with bone to foot short and strong.

The hindlegs are parallel when viewed from behind.

The wording of the three Standards differs, but the intent is the same in each case. Well-laid forequarters are the key to proper conformation in the Bully. The broad shoulder blades should be firmly attached to the rib cage and well laid back, forming almost a right angle with the upper arm. In the author's experience, even with well-laid shoulders, this angle is rarely close to 90 degrees, more typically being 100 degrees or more. Be that as it may, correct conformation here leads to an ample forechest with the elbows placed well back and tucked into the chest.

Forelegs should be straight, viewed from any angle; the term 'gun barrel' often being applied to the ideal here. Equally, the pasterns should be strong and upright, adding to the gun barrel straightness. The strong, round bone should not be in any way coarse, quality being the operative word. Of course, the bone itself is not actually round, but appears so to the touch.

Moving on to the Bully's hindquarters, the correct angles and proportions are most important; also, though not stated, they should balance the forequarters. Parallel when viewed from behind, the hindlegs should sport broad, muscular thighs and

AKC

Legs: Should be big boned but not to the point of coarseness; the forelegs should be of moderate length, perfectly straight, and the dog must stand firmly upon them. The elbows must turn neither in nor out, and the pasterns should be strong and upright. The hind legs should be parallel viewed from behind. The thighs very muscular with hocks well let down. Hind pasterns short and upright. The stifle joint should be well bent with a well-developed second thigh.

FCI

Limbs: Forequarters: Forelegs have strongest type of round, quality bone; dog should stand

solidly upon them and they should be perfectly parallel. In mature dogs length of forelegs should be approximately equal to depth of chest. Shoulders: Strong and muscular without loading. Shoulder blades wide, flat and held closely to chest wall and have a very pronounced backward slope of front edge from bottom to top, forming almost a right angle with upper arm. Elbows: Held straight and strong. Pasterns: Upright. Hindquarters: Hindlegs parallel when viewed from behind. Thighs: Muscular. Stifle: Joint well bent. Second thighs: Well developed. Hock: Well angulated. Metatarsus: With bone to foot short and strong.

well-developed second thighs, well-bent stifles and short, strong hocks that are well angulated. The AKC still uses the old term 'well let down' for the hocks, but the meaning is exactly the same. In the show ring, straight stifles are not unusual and hocks are rarely as short as desired.

A tendency towards loaded shoulders and a Queen Anne – rather than gun barrel – shape to the front legs and pasterns point to the Bull Terrier's Bulldog heritage. These are serious faults and extremely difficult to eradicate from a breeding programme.

FEET

KC and FCI
Feet: Round and compact with well arched toes.

AKC
Feet: Round and compact with well-arched toes like a cat.

Brief and to the point, the feet should be truly cat-like with thick pads, well suited to carrying a relatively heavy dog in its athletic pursuits. The Standards don't mention that the feet should be comparatively small, with the rear feet usually slightly smaller than the fronts. Splayed and thin feet are anathema. An old expression

The tail should be thick at the root, tapering to a fine point. It should be carried horizontally. *Alice van Kempen*

tells us: God makes Bull Terriers; breeders (or owners) make feet – meaning exercise on suitable surfaces and periodic trimming of nails, though the more correct the feet, the less attention they need.

TAIL

KC and FCI
Tail: Short, set on low and carried horizontally. Thick at root, it tapers to a fine point.

AKC
Tail: Should be short, set on low, fine, and ideally should be carried horizontally. It should be thick where it joins the body, and should taper to a fine point.

For the tail, just remember: short and set low on the croup. The fall off at the croup completes the overall flow of the topline – from withers set well back, flat in the middle, slight rise over loins falling away to the low-set tail. The tail should be carried horizontally, though a Bully will tend to carry it higher when excited. But the tail must not be set gaily, as with many of the terriers. This ruins the lines of a Bully and indicates that the angle of the pelvis is wrong.

GAIT/ MOVEMENT

KC and FCI
Gait/Movement: When moving appears well knit, smoothly covering ground with free, easy strides and with a typical jaunty air. When trotting, movement parallel, front and back, only converging towards centre line at faster speeds, forelegs reaching out well and hindlegs moving smoothly at hip, flexing well at stifle and hock, with great thrust.

AKC
Movement: The dog shall move smoothly, covering the ground with free, easy strides, fore and hind legs should move parallel each to each when viewed from

in front or behind. The forelegs reaching out well and the hind legs moving smoothly at the hip and flexing well at the stifle and hock. The dog should move compactly and in one piece but with a typical jaunty air that suggests agility and power.

The KC and AKC wordings differ, but again there is no difference in intent. Discussion of gait often starts out with the statement that movement is the crucial test of conformation. And, of course, this is true. A good handler might be able to stack a poorly made dog to look impressive, but, once on the move, the dog's faulty construction will soon become apparent. A Bully should move with free, easy strides and a jaunty air. This jauntiness is characteristic of the breed, stemming from the Bully's broad chest and general muscularity. As the AKC Standard notes, this jauntiness suggests power and agility; a Bully should be agile. Also the legs should remain parallel whether viewed from in front or behind. Although there is no mention of it, the topline should hold on the move, without slackness – a dip behind the withers – or roach. Both KC and AKC Standards call for the

The Bull Terrier should move with free, easy strides.

Bully to reach well out in front and flex well behind. A Bully with less spring of rib and longer in loin will tend to move more freely and smoothly, losing some of that jauntiness. This is not correct conformation or movement and should be faulted.

Movement should be assessed from the side as well as coming and going with the Bully handled on a loose leash; the Bully should not be strung up. Common faults in the breed include restricted reach in front, also paddling (front legs swinging stiffly forwards and outwards in an arc), lack of flex and drive behind, and cow hocks (where the hocks turn in, usually accompanied by the rear feet toeing out).

COAT

KC
Coat: Short, flat, even and harsh to touch with a fine gloss. Skin fitting dog tightly. A soft textured undercoat may be present in winter.

AKC
Coat: Should be short, flat, harsh to the touch and with a fine gloss. The dog's skin should fit tightly.

FCI
Skin: Fitting dog tightly. Hair: Short, flat, even and harsh to touch with a fine gloss. A soft textured undercoat may be present in winter.

The three Standards agree that the coat should be short, flat and harsh to the touch. The gloss or gleam, which is more readily apparent in the coloured coats, points to the overall health and condition of the dog. Although not mentioned, Bull Terriers can grow a softer undercoat and most grow much heavier coats in winter conditions. The excess coat is cast in the spring and it is then that ticking can appear – small coloured patches among the white hairs. These are undesirable but not considered a major fault, as discussed in the next section.

BULL TERRIER COLOURS

Pure white Bull Terriers.

Alice van Kempen.

There may be patches of colour on the head.

Alice van Kempen.

Black brindle with white markings.

Alice van Kempen.

The brindle markings may be on a paler background.

The rich colouring of a red dog.   *Alice van Kempen.*

The striking markings of
a tricolour.   *Alice van Kempen.*

A fawn dog is much lighter in colour.   *Alice van Kempen.*

COLOUR

KC and FCI

Colour: For White, pure white coat. Skin pigmentation and markings on head not to be penalised. For Coloured, colour predominates; all other things being equal, brindle preferred. Black, brindle, red, fawn and tricolour acceptable. Tick markings in white coat undesirable. Blue and liver highly undesirable.

AKC

White: Color: Is white though markings on the head are permissible. Any markings elsewhere on the coat are to be severely faulted. Skin pigmentation is not to be penalized.
Colored: The Standard for the Colored Variety is the same as for the White except for the sub head 'Color' which reads: Color. Any color other than white, or any color with white markings. Other things being equal, the preferred color is brindle. A dog which is predominantly white shall be disqualified.

Bull Terriers come in two hues – white and coloured. The whites are not albinos; they are coloured dogs in which much of the colour has been inhibited. Patches of coloured hair often occur on the head, particularly around the eyes and ears. These markings are permissible, but any behind the collar are to be faulted. The AKC Standard required the disqualification of dogs with such markings until 1968; now they are simply a fault. Many breeders consider such faults to be cosmetic and not as serious as, for example, constructional problems. Markings in the coat must not be confused with skin pigmentation, which is not penalised and, in fact, should be welcomed from the viewpoint of genetics and health. The seasonal tick markings sported by some dogs are undesirable, but not a serious fault. Mention of ticking was eliminated from the AKC Standard, as some judges confused these marks with skin pigmentation and wrongly penalised dogs.

Coloured Bull Terriers are considered a separate variety of the breed only in America and, of course, they differ from the whites only in the colour of their coats. There are no requirements for the pattern on coloureds, only that colour predominates, which is usually interpreted as more than 50 per cent of the coat is coloured. Some coloureds are termed solids; this means they have very little white on them, though there is always some. Most coloureds are flash marked – or Irish-spotted as we used to call it – with a white blaze on the muzzle, a white collar around the neck, white socks and a white tip to the tail. There are, however, considerable variations in the actual markings; for example, the size and placement of the blaze and the width of the collar and whether it is complete or not. The acceptable colours are brindle, black brindle (black with brindle showing around the edges), any shade of red through fawn – all of course with some white coat – and finally tricolour (black, tan and white). The preference for brindle has a long standing in the breed, but it is preferred only if everything else is equal, which is rarely, if ever, the case.

More recently, the AKC and FCI Standards were updated to state that blue and liver are highly undesirable colours. Blue is a dilution of the usual black colour in the coat and the nose while liver results in a liver-coloured nose and lighter brown eyes. In America these changes were considered unnecessary, as the results should be faulted according to the Standard, which requires very dark eyes and a black nose.

When judging Bull Terriers it is important to be aware of the potential for optical illusions. Colour markings on the head can add or detract from the profile; dark colours on the muzzle can result in the illusion of less fill under the eyes; the width of the white collar can give the impression of the neck being longer or shorter than it actually is, and so on.

SIZE

KC and FCI

Size: There are neither weight nor height limits, but there should be the impression of maximum substance for size of dog consistent with quality and sex.

There is a wide variation in size among Bull Terriers. *Alice van Kempen.*

AKC
No comments.

'Maximum substance for size of dog consistent with quality and sex' – that says it all. There are no size restrictions on Bull Terriers, just these guidelines – a lot of dog for the size of the frame yet without even a hint of coarseness. The AKC Standard makes no specific reference to size, but the same guidelines are implied.

Bull Terriers have always ranged widely in size, but there can be no doubt that our dogs have become progressively bigger, certainly heavier. A few decades ago, a typical male might weigh 30 kg or less; today we find many winning males who weigh in at 35 kg or more. Bitches, of course, weigh less on average, but they too have gained in size. In America, to a certain degree, there is a 'bigger is better'

syndrome at play, and in response a number of established breeders are now consciously trying to bring down the size of their dogs. The old adage that a big'un always beats a little'un does not apply. There is also an argument that the very small Bully tends to lose substance and become more terrier-like, while a very large Bully tends to fail in shapeliness and sometimes compactness. The winner should always be the dog that best meets the definition of the perfect Bully defined in the Standard, regardless of size.

FAULTS

KC and FCI
Faults: Any departure from the foregoing points should be considered a fault and the seriousness with which the fault should be regarded should be in exact proportion to its

degree and its effect upon the health and welfare of the dog.

AKC
Faults: Any departure from the foregoing points shall be considered a fault and the seriousness of the fault shall be in exact proportion to its degree, i.e. a very crooked front is a very bad fault; a rather crooked front is a rather bad fault; and a slightly crooked front is a slight fault.

The Standards are the same, except for the AKC providing an example. Each fault should be considered in proportion to its degree; it's as simple as that. Remember here that the Standard is a positive statement of the virtues of the Bull Terrier. Deviations from the Standards are faults of varying degrees of seriousness. These faults should be balanced against a Bully's virtues. A lack of faults does not indicate a presence of outstanding virtues; a faultless dog may be a nonentity in terms of breed virtues. It is these virtues that will progress the breed.

NOTES AND DISQUALIFICATIONS

KC
Note: Male animals should have two apparently normal testicles fully descended into the scrotum.

AKC
Disqualification (White): Blue eyes. Disqualifications

(Colored): Blue eyes. Any dog which is predominantly white.

FCI
Any dog clearly showing physical or behavioural abnormalities shall be disqualified. N.B.: Male animals should have two apparently normal testicles fully descended into the scrotum.

A Bull Terrier requires minimal grooming for the show ring, but he should be in hard, muscular condition.

The KC has moved away from disqualifications, preferring to apply the description 'highly undesirable' to faults that were previously disqualified. On the other hand, both the AKC and the FCI have retained them. The AKC Standard requires Bull Terriers with blue eyes to be disqualified, also any coloured that is predominantly white. The FCI Standard alone disqualifies a dog with clear abnormalities, a laudable addition to the Standard.

Both the KC and the FCI state that males should have two normal and full descended testicles, whereas the AKC does not refer to testicles in individual Standards. Instead, the AKC applies this statement to all breeds: '... a male which does not have two normal testicles normally located in the scrotum may not compete at any show and will be disqualified...'

PRESENTATION

The essentials for presenting a Bull Terrier in the show ring are straightforward, with minimal grooming needed. Most importantly, your Bully should be really well exercised to ensure that hard muscle tone and correct weight. He must be in tip-top health to secure that gleaming coat and alert general appearance. It is usual to cut off the whiskers, thus smoothing the lines of the egg-shaped head, and to trim the end and underneath of the tail to neaten its appearance. Exhibitors used to trim much of the hair off the inside of the ears, but few do so today.

In days of yore it was not unusual for a Bully to swagger into the ring, shaking off an impressive cloud of white chalk. This is no longer permitted – changing the appearance of a dog with a foreign substance is banned. However, exhibitors in most countries still employ whitening agents to enhance the appearance of their white Bull Terriers and the white parts of the coloureds, especially around the muzzle. The trick is to rub in white make-up, apply the chalk judiciously and then to remove it. Well, not quite all of it; just enough so that it isn't too noticeable and doesn't come off on the hands of the judge.

The vast majority of Bull Terriers are shown by their owners, though a number of top winners in America are now handled by professionals. While there are exceptions, most of us don't do a very good job of showing our own dogs. The early training of a puppy for the ring is advantageous. Both handler and dog need to be familiar and comfortable with what to do. The Bully is typically shown on a loose leash, as stringing them up tends to detract rather than to help. The key is for both handler and dog to work as a team and to enjoy what they are doing.

HAPPY AND HEALTHY

Chapter

Bull Terriers are stoical dogs with a life span that can run well into double figures. Although he has many of the terrier traits one would expect, the Bull Terrier is renowned as a plucky, faithful companion and a willing friend on a non-conditional basis. He will, however, of necessity rely on you for food and shelter, accident prevention and medication. A healthy Bull Terrier is a happy chap, looking to please and amuse his owner.

Some of my best memories associated with my grandmother centre around her last Bull Terrier. Suzie was very bouncy indeed, to the extent that I had to stand outside the front wall of the garden and hope that my grandmother was at the front window so that I could wave and catch her attention. There was no way I could open the gate and

walk across the lawn to the front door, because Suzie would appear as if from nowhere and launch herself at me, which was quite alarming for a child! Once I had been greeted, though, she was a great dog – such a character.

There are only a few genetic conditions as yet recognised in the Bull Terrier, which will be covered in depth later in the chapter.

ROUTINE HEALTH CARE

VACCINATION
There is much debate over the issue of vaccination at the moment. The timing of the final part of the initial vaccination course for a puppy and the frequency of subsequent booster vaccinations are both under scrutiny. An evaluation of the relative risk for each disease plays a part, depending on the local situation.

Many owners think that the actual vaccination is the protection, so that their puppy can go out for walks as soon as he or she has had the final part of the puppy vaccination course. This is not the case. The rationale behind vaccination is to stimulate the immune system into producing protective antibodies, which will be triggered if the patient is subsequently exposed to that particular disease. This means that a further one or two weeks will have to pass before an effective level of protection will have developed.

Vaccines against viruses stimulate longer-lasting protection than those against bacteria, whose effect may only persist for a matter of months in some cases. There is also the possibility of an individual failing to mount a full immune response to a vaccination: although the vaccine schedule may have been

Your vet will advise on the best time to start a vaccination programme.
Alice van Kempen.

followed as recommended, that particular dog remains vulnerable.

A dog's level of protection against rabies, as demonstrated by the antibody titre in a blood sample, is routinely tested in the UK in order to fulfil the requirements of the Pet Travel Scheme (PETS). This is not required at the current time with any other individual diseases in order to gauge the need for booster vaccination or to determine the effect of a course of vaccines; instead, your veterinary surgeon will advise a protocol based upon the vaccines available, local disease prevalence, and the lifestyle of you and your dog.

It is worth remembering that maintaining a fully effective level

of immune protection against the disease appropriate to your locale is vital: these are serious diseases, which may result in the death of your dog, and some may have the potential to be passed on to his human family (so-called zoonotic potential for transmission). This is where you will be grateful for your veterinary surgeon's own knowledge and advice.

The American Animal Hospital Association laid down guidance at the end of 2006 for the vaccination of dogs in North America. Core diseases were defined as distemper, adenovirus, parvovirus and rabies. So-called non-core diseases are kennel cough, Lyme disease and leptospirosis. A decision to vaccinate against one or more

non-core diseases will be based on an individual's level of risk, determined on lifestyle and where you live in the US.

Do remember, however, that the booster visit to the veterinary surgery is not 'just' for a booster. I am regularly correcting my clients when they announce that they have 'just' brought their pet for a booster. Instead, this appointment is a chance for a full health check and evaluation of how a particular dog is doing. After all, we are all conversant with the adage that a human year is equivalent to seven canine years.

There have been attempts in recent times to reset the scale for two reasons: small breeds live longer than giant breeds, and dogs are living longer than previously. I have seen dogs of 17 and 18 years of age, but to say a dog is 119 or 126 years old is plainly meaningless. It does emphasise the fact, though, that a dog's health can change dramatically over the course of a single year, because dogs age at a far faster rate than humans.

For me as a veterinary surgeon, the booster vaccination visit is a challenge: how much can I find of which the owner was unaware, such as rotten teeth or a heart murmur? Even monitoring bodyweight year upon year is of use, because bodyweight can creep up, or down, without an owner realising. Being overweight is unhealthy, but it may take an outsider's remark to make an owner realise that there is a problem. Conversely, a drop in

Kennel cough is highly contagious and will spread rapidly among dogs that live together. *Alice van Kempen.*

bodyweight may be the only pointer to an underlying problem.

The diseases against which dogs are vaccinted include:

ADENOVIRUS

Canine adenovirus 1 (CAV-1) affects the liver (hepatitis) and is seen within affected dogs as the classic 'blue eye', while CAV-2 is a cause of kennel cough (see later). Vaccines often include both canine adenoviruses.

DISTEMPER

This disease is sometimes called 'hardpad' from the characteristic changes to the pads of the paws. It has a worldwide distribution, but fortunately vaccination has been very effective at reducing its occurrence. It is caused by a virus and affects the respiratory, gastro-intestinal (gut) and nervous systems, so it causes a wide range of illnesses. Fox and urban stray dog populations are most at risk and are usually responsible for local outbreaks.

KENNEL COUGH

Also known as infectious tracheobronchitis, Bordetella bronchiseptica is not only a major cause of kennel cough but also a common secondary infection on top of another cause. Being a bacterium, it is susceptible to treatment with appropriate antibiotics, but the immunity stimulated by the vaccine is therefore short-lived (six to 12 months).

This vaccine is often in a form to be administered down the nostrils in order to stimulate local immunity at the point of entry, so to speak. Do not be alarmed to see your veterinary surgeon using a needle and syringe to draw up the vaccine, because the needle will be replaced with a special plastic introducer, allowing the vaccine to be gently instilled into each nostril. Dogs generally resent being held more than the actual intra-nasal vaccine, and I have learnt that covering the patient's eyes helps greatly.

Kennel cough is, however, rather a catch-all term for any cough spreading within a dog population – not just in kennels, but also between dogs at a training session or breed show, or even mixing in the park. Many of these infections may not be B. bronchiseptica but other viruses, for which one can only treat symptomatically. Parainfluenza virus is often included in a vaccine programme, as it is a common viral cause of kennel cough.

LEPTOSPIROSIS

This disease is caused by Leptospira interogans, a spiral-shaped bacterium. There are several natural variants or serovars. Each is characteristically found in one or more particular host animal species, which then acts as a reservoir, intermittently shedding leptospires in the urine. Infection can also be picked up at mating, via bite wounds, across the placenta, or through eating the carcases of infected animals (such as rats).

A serovar will cause actual clinical disease in an individual when two conditions are fulfilled: the individual is not the natural host species, and is also not immune to that particular serovar.

Leptospirosis is a zoonotic disease, known as Weil's disease in humans, with implications for all those in contact with an affected dog. It is also commonly called rat jaundice, reflecting the rat's important role as a carrier. The UK National Rodent Survey 2003 found a wild brown rat population of 60 million, equivalent at the time to one rat per person. Wherever you live in the UK, rats are endemic, which means that there is as much a risk to the Bull Terrier living with a family in a town as the Bull Terrier leading a rural lifestyle.

Signs of illness reflect the organs affected by a particular serovar. In humans, there may be a flu-like illness or a more serious, often life-threatening disorder involving major body organs. The illness in a susceptible dog may be mild, the dog recovering within two to three weeks without treatment but going on to develop long-term liver or kidney disease. In contrast, peracute illness may result in a rapid deterioration and death following an initial malaise and fever. There may also be anorexia, vomiting, diarrhoea, abdominal pain, joint pain, increased thirst and urination rate, jaundice, and ocular changes. Haemorrhage is also a common feature, manifesting as bleeding under the skin, nosebleeds, and the presence of blood in the urine and faeces.

Treatment requires rigorous intravenous fluid therapy to support the kidneys. Being a bacterial infection, it is possible to treat leptospirosis with specific antibiotics, although a prolonged course of several weeks is needed. Strict hygiene and barrier nursing are required in order to avoid onward transmission of the disease.

Annual vaccination is recommended for leptospirosis because the immunity only lasts for a year, unlike the longer immunity associated with vaccines against viruses. There is, however, little or no cross-protection between Leptospira serovars, so vaccination will result in protection against only those serovars included in the particular vaccine used. Additionally, although vaccination against leptospirosis will prevent active disease if an individual is exposed to a serovar included in the vaccine, it cannot prevent infection of that individual and becoming a carrier in the long-term.

In the UK, vaccines have classically included L icterohaemorrhagiae (rat-adapted serovar) and L canicola (dog-specific serovar). The latter is of especial significance to us humans, since disease will not be apparent in an infected dog but leptospires will be shed intermittently.

Kennel cough can seem alarming. There is a persistent cough accompanied by the production of white frothy spittle, which can last for a matter of weeks; during this time the patient is highly infectious to other dogs. I remember when it ran through our five Border Collies – there were white patches of froth on the floor wherever you looked! Other features include sneezing, a runny nose, and eyes sore with conjunctivitis.

Fortunately, these infections are generally self-limiting, most dogs recovering without any long-lasting problems, but an elderly dog may be knocked sideways by it, akin to the effects of a common cold on a frail, elderly person.

LYME DISEASE

This is a bacterial infection transmitted by hard ticks. It is restricted to those specific areas of the US where ticks are found, such as the north-eastern states, some southern states, California and the upper Mississippi region. It does also occur in the UK, but at a low level, so vaccination is not routinely offered.

Clinical disease is manifested primarily as limping due to arthritis, but other organs affected include the heart, kidneys and nervous system. It is readily treatable with appropriate antibiotics, once diagnosed, but the causal bacterium, Borrelia burgdorferi, is not cleared from the body totally and will persist. Prevention requires both vaccination and tick control, especially as there are other diseases transmitted by ticks. Ticks carrying B. burgdorferi will transmit it to humans as well, but an infected dog cannot pass it to a human.

Lyme disease is a tick-borne disease. Fortunately, it is still rare in the UK.
Alice van Kempen.

PARVOVIRUS (CPV)

Canine parvovirus disease first appeared in the late 1970s, when it was feared that the UK's dog population would be decimated by it because of the lack of immunity in the general canine population. While this was a terrifying possibility at the time, fortunately it did not happen.

There are two forms of the virus (CPV-1, CPV-2) affecting domesticated dogs. It is highly contagious, picked up via the mouth/nose from infected faeces. The incubation period is about five days. CPV-2 causes two types of illness: gastro-enteritis and heart disease in puppies born to unvaccinated dams, both of which often result in death. Infection of puppies under three weeks of age with CPV-1 manifests as diarrhoea, vomiting, difficulty breathing, and fading puppy syndrome. CPV-1 can cause abortion and foetal abnormalities in breeding bitches.

Occurrence is mainly low now, thanks to vaccination, although a recent outbreak in my area did claim the lives of several dogs. It is also occasionally seen in the elderly unvaccinated dog.

RABIES

This is another zoonotic disease and there are very strict control measures in place. Vaccines were once available in the UK only on an individual basis for dogs being taken abroad. Pets travelling into the UK had to serve six months' compulsory quarantine so that any pet incubating rabies would be identified before release back into the general population. Under the Pet Travel Scheme (PETS), provided certain criteria are met (check the DEFRA website for up-to-date information – www.defra.gov.uk) then dogs can re-enter the UK without being quarantined.

Dogs to be imported into the US have to show that they were vaccinated against rabies at least 30 days previously; otherwise, they have to serve effective internal quarantine for 30 days from the date of vaccination against rabies, in order to ensure they are not incubating rabies. The exception is dogs entering from countries recognised as being rabies-free, in which case it has to be proved that they lived in that country for at least six months beforehand.

All puppies should be routinely treated for roundworm.

Alice van Kempen.

PARASITES

A parasite is defined as an organism deriving benefit on a one-way basis from another, the host. It goes without saying that it is not to the parasite's advantage to harm the host to such an extent that the benefit is lost, especially if it results in the death of the host. This means a dog could harbour parasites, internal and/or external, without there being any signs apparent to the owner. Many canine parasites can, however, transfer to humans with variable consequences, so routine preventative treatment is advised against particular parasites.

Just as with vaccination, risk assessment plays a part – for example, there is no need for routine heartworm treatment in the UK (at present), but it is vital in the US and in Mediterranean countries.

ROUNDWORMS (NEMATODES)

These are the spaghetti-like worms that you may have seen passed in faeces or brought up in vomit. Most of the deworming treatments in use today cause the adult roundworms to disintegrate, thankfully, so that treating puppies in particular is not as unpleasant as it used to be!

Most puppies will have a worm burden, mainly of a particular roundworm species (Toxocara canis), which reactivates within the dam's tissues during pregnancy and passes to the foetuses developing in the womb. It is therefore important to treat the dam both during and after pregnancy, as well as the puppies.

Professional advice is to continue worming every one to three months. There are roundworm eggs in the environment and, unless you examine your dog's faeces under a microscope on a very regular basis for the presence of roundworm eggs, you will be unaware of your dog having picked up roundworms, unless he should have such a heavy burden that he passes the adults.

It takes a few weeks from the time that a dog swallows a Toxocara canis roundworm egg to himself passing viable eggs (the pre-patent period). These eggs are not immediately infective to other animals, requiring a period of maturation in the environment, which is primarily temperature-dependent and therefore shorter in the summer (as little as two weeks) than in the winter. The eggs can survive in the environment for two years and more.

There are deworming products that are active all the time, which will provide continuous protection when administered as often as directed. Otherwise, treating every month will, in effect, cut in before a dog could theoretically become a source of roundworm eggs to the general population.

It is the risk to human health that is so important: T. canis roundworms will migrate within our tissues and cause all manner of problems, not least of which (but fortunately rarely) is blindness. If a dog has roundworms, the eggs also find their way on to his coat where they can be picked up during stroking. Sensible hygiene is therefore important. You should always carefully pick up your dog's faeces and dispose of them appropriately, thereby preventing the maturation of any eggs present in the fresh faeces.

HEARTWORM (DIROFILARIA IMMITIS)

Heartworm infection has been diagnosed in dogs all over the world. There are two prerequisites: the presence of mosquitoes, and a warm, humid climate.

When a female mosquito bites an infected animal, it acquires D. immitis in its circulating form, as microfilariae. A warm environmental temperature is needed for these microfilariae to

TAPEWORMS (CESTODES)

When considering the general dog population, the primary source of the commonest tapeworm species will be fleas, which can carry the eggs. Most multi-wormers will be active against these tapeworms. They are not a threat to human health, but it is unpleasant to see the wriggly ricegrain tapeworm segments emerging from your dog's back passage while he is lying in front of the fire, and usually when you have guests for dinner!

A tapeworm of significance to human health is Echinococcus granulosus, found in a few parts of the UK, mainly in Wales. Man is an intermediate host for this tapeworm, along with sheep, cattle and pigs. Inadvertent ingestion of eggs passed in the faeces of an infected dog is followed by the development of so-called hydatid cysts in major organs, such as the lungs and liver, necessitating surgical removal. Dogs become infected through eating raw meat containing hydatid cysts. Cooking will kill hydatid cysts, so avoid feeding raw meat and offal in areas of high risk.

There are specific requirements for treatment with praziquantel within 24 to 48 hours of return into the UK under the PETS. This is to prevent the inadvertent introduction of Echinococcus multilocularis, a tapeworm carried by foxes on mainland Europe, which is transmissible to humans, causing serious or even fatal liver disease.

develop into the infective third-stage larvae (L3) within the mosquitoes, the so-called intermediate host. L3 larvae are then transmitted by the mosquito when it next bites a dog. Therefore, while heartworm infection is found in all parts of the United States, it is at differing levels. An occurrence in Alaska, for example, is probably a reflection of a visiting dog having previously picked up the infection elsewhere.

Heartworm infection is not currently a problem in the UK, except for those dogs contracting it while abroad without suitable preventative treatment. Global warming and its effect on the UK's climate, however, could change that.

It is a potentially life-threatening condition, with dogs of all breeds and ages being susceptible without preventative treatment. The larvae can grow to 14 inches within the right side of the heart, causing primarily signs of heart failure and ultimately liver and kidney damage. It can be treated but prevention is a better plan. In the US, regular blood tests for the presence of infection are advised, coupled with appropriate preventative measures, so I would advise liaison with your veterinary surgeon.

For dogs travelling to heartworm-endemic areas of the EU, such as the Mediterranean coast, preventative treatment should be started before leaving the UK and maintained during the visit. Again, this is best arranged with your veterinary surgeon.

Spot-on treatment is effective in controlling fleas.

FLEAS

There are several species of flea, which are not host-specific. A dog can be carrying cat and human fleas as well as dog fleas, but the same flea treatment will kill and/or control them all. It is also accepted that environmental control is a vital part of a flea control programme. This is because the adult flea is only on the animal for as long as it takes to have a blood meal and to breed; the remainder of the life cycle occurs in the house, car, caravan, shed…

There is a vast array of flea control products available, with various routes of administration: collar, powder, spray, 'spot-on', or oral. Flea control needs to be applied to all pets in the house, regardless of whether they leave the house, since fleas can be introduced into the home by other pets and their human owners. Discuss your specific flea control needs with your veterinary surgeon.

MITES

There are five types of mite that can affect dogs.

Demodex canis: This mite is a normal inhabitant of canine hair follicles, passed from the bitch to her pups as they suckle. The development of actual skin disease or demodicosis depends on the individual. It is seen frequently around the time of puberty and after a bitch's first season, associated with hormonal changes. There may, however, be an inherited weakness in an individual's immune system, enabling multiplication of the mite.

The localised form consists of areas of fur loss without itchiness, generally around the face and on the forelimbs, and 90 per cent will recover without treatment. The other 10 per cent develop the juvenile-onset generalised form, of which half will recover spontaneously. The other half may be depressed, go off their food, and show signs of itchiness due to secondary bacterial skin infections.

Treatment is often prolonged over several months and consists of regular bathing with a specific miticidal shampoo, often clipping away fur to improve access to the skin, together with a suitable antibiotic by mouth. There is also now a licensed 'spot-on' preparation available. Progress is monitored by the examination of deep skin scrapings for the presence of the mite; the initial diagnosis is based upon abnormally high numbers of the mite, often with live individuals being seen.

Some Bull Terriers may develop demodicosis for the first time in middle-age (more than four years of age). This often reflects underlying immunosuppression by an internal disease, so it is

It is easier to keep a check for external parasites on a short-coated breed.
Alice van Kempen.

important to identify such a cause and correct it where possible, as well as treating the skin condition.

Sarcoptes scabei: This characteristically causes an intense pruritus or itchiness in the affected Bull Terrier, causing him to incessantly scratch and bite at himself, leading to marked fur loss and skin trauma. Initially starting on the elbows, earflaps and hocks, without treatment the skin on the rest of the body can become affected, with thickening and pigmentation of the skin. Secondary bacterial infections are common.

Unlike Demodex, this mite lives at the skin surface, and it can be hard to find in skin scrapings. It is therefore not unusual to treat a patient for sarcoptic mange (scabies) based on the appearance of the problem even with negative skin scraping findings, and especially if there is a history of contact with foxes, which are a frequent source of the scabies mite.

It will spread between dogs and can therefore also be found in situations where large numbers of dogs from different backgrounds are mixing together. It will cause itchiness in humans, although the mite cannot complete its life cycle on us, so treating all affected dogs should be sufficient. Fortunately, there is now a highly effective 'spot-on' treatment for Sarcoptes scabei.

Cheyletiella yasguri: This is the fur mite most commonly found on dogs. It is often called 'walking dandruff' because it can be possible to see collections of the small white mite moving about over the skin surface. There is excessive scale and dandruff formation, and mild itchiness. It is transmissible to humans, causing a pruritic rash.

Diagnosis is by microscopic examination of skin scrapings, coat combings and sticky tape impressions from the skin and fur. Treatment is with an appropriate insecticide, as advised by your veterinary surgeon.

Otodectes cynotis: A highly transmissible otitis externa (outer ear infection) results from the presence in the outer ear canal of this ear mite, characterised by exuberant production of dark earwax. The patient will frequently shake his head and rub at the ear(s) affected. The mites can also spread on to the skin adjacent to the opening of the external ear canal, and may transfer elsewhere, such as to the paws.

TICKS

Ticks have become an increasing problem in recent years throughout Britain. Their physical presence causes irritation, but it is their potential to spread disease that causes concern. A tick will transmit any infection previously contracted while feeding on an animal: for example Borrelia burgdorferi, the causal agent of Lyme disease (see page 132).

The life cycle of the tick is curious: each life stage takes a year to develop and move on to the next. Long grass is a major habitat. The vibration of animals moving through the grass will stimulate the larva, nymph or adult to climb up a blade of grass and wave its legs in the air as it 'quests' for a host on to which to latch for its next blood meal. Humans are as likely to be hosts, so ramblers and orienteers are advised to cover their legs when going through rough long grass.

Removing a tick is simple – provided your dog will stay still. The important rule is to twist gently so that the tick is persuaded to let go with its mouthparts. Grasp the body of the tick as near to your dog's skin as possible, either between thumb and fingers or with a specific tick-removing instrument, and then rotate in one direction until the tick comes away. I keep a plastic tick hook in my wallet at all times.

When using an otoscope to examine the outer ear canal, the heat from the light source will often cause any ear mites present to start moving around. I often offer owners the chance to have a look, because it really is quite an extraordinary sight! It is also possible to identify the mite from earwax smeared on to a slide and examined under a microscope.

Cats are a common source of ear mites. It is not unusual to find ear mites during the routine examination of puppies and kittens. Treatment options include specific eardrops acting against both the mite and any secondary infections present in the auditory canal, and certain 'spot-on' formulations. It is vital to treat all dogs and cats in the household to prevent recycling of the mite between individuals.

(Neo-) Trombicula autumnalis: The free-living harvest mite can cause an intense local irritation on the skin. Its larvae are picked up from undergrowth, so they are characteristically found as a bright orange patch on the web of skin between the digits of the paws. It feeds on skin cells before dropping off to complete its life cycle in the environment.

Its name is a little misleading, because it is not restricted to the autumn nor to harvest-time; I find it on the earflaps of cats from late June onwards, depending on the prevailing weather. It will also bite humans.

Treatment depends on identifying and avoiding hotspots for picking up harvest mites, if possible. Checking the skin, especially the paws, after exercise and mechanically removing any mites found will reduce the chances of irritation, which can be treated symptomatically. Insecticides can also be applied – be guided by your veterinary surgeon.

A-Z OF COMMON AILMENTS

ANAL SACS, IMPACTED

The anal sacs lie on either side of the anus at approximately four and eight o'clock, if compared with the face of a clock. They fill with a particularly pungent fluid, which is emptied on to the faeces as they move past the sacs to exit from the anus. Theories abound as to why these sacs should become impacted periodically and seemingly more so in some dogs than others.

The irritation of impacted anal sacs is often seen as 'scooting', when the backside is dragged along the ground. Some dogs will also gnaw at their back feet or over the rump. I certainly remember Suzie crossing the dining room carpet on her backside!

Increasing the fibre content of the diet helps some dogs; in others, there is underlying skin disease. It may be a one-off occurrence for no apparent reason. Sometimes an infection can become established, requiring antibiotic therapy, which may need to be coupled with flushing out the infected sac under sedation or general anaesthesia. More rarely, a dog will present with an apparently acute-onset anal sac abscess, which is incredibly painful.

DIARRHOEA
Cause and treatment much as Gastritis (see below).

EAR INFECTIONS
The dog has a long external ear canal, initially vertical then horizontal, leading to the eardrum, which protects the middle ear. If your Bull Terrier is shaking his head, then his ears will need to be inspected with an auroscope by a veterinary surgeon in order to identify any cause, and to ensure the eardrum is intact. A sample may be taken from the canal to be examined under the microscope and cultured, to identify causal agents before prescribing appropriate eardrops containing antibiotic, antifungal agent and/or steroid. Predisposing causes of otitis externa or infection in the external ear canal include:
- Presence of a foreign body, such as a grass awn
- Ear mites, which are intensely irritating to the dog and stimulate the production of brown wax, predisposing to infection

The erect ear carriage of a Bull Terrier aids air circulation and means that the breed is less prone to ear infections. *Alice van Kempen.*

- Previous infections, causing the canal's lining to thicken, narrowing the canal and reducing ventilation
- Swimming – some Bull Terriers will swim, but water trapped in the external ear canal can lead to infection, especially if the water is not clean.

FOREIGN BODIES
- **Internal:** Items swallowed in haste without checking whether they will be digested can cause problems if they lodge in the stomach or obstruct the intestines, necessitating surgical removal. Acute vomiting is the main indication. Common objects I have seen removed include stones from the garden, peach stones, babies' dummies, golf balls, and, once, a lady's bra… It is possible to diagnose a dog with an intestinal obstruction across a waiting room from a particularly 'tucked-up' stance and pained facial expression. These patients bounce back from surgery dramatically. A previously docile and compliant obstructed patient will return for a post-operative check-up and literally bounce into the consulting room.
- **External:** Grass awns are adept at finding their way into orifices such as a nostril, down an ear, and into the soft skin between two digits (toes), whence they start a one-way

Dogs are natural scavengers, and this can lead to gastric upset.
Alice van Kempen.

journey due to the direction of their whiskers. In particular, I remember a grass awn that migrated from a hindpaw, causing abscesses along the way but not yielding itself up until it erupted through the skin in the groin!

GASTRITIS
This is usually a simple stomach upset, most commonly in response to dietary indiscretion. Scavenging constitutes a change in the diet as much as an abrupt switch in the food being fed by the owner. I particularly remember how, on Easter Sundays, Suzie would attempt to steal our chocolate Easter eggs the moment our backs were turned (not forgetting that the theobromine in chocolate poses a health risk to dogs in its own right).

There are also some specific infections causing more severe gastritis/enteritis, which will require treatment from a veterinary surgeon (see also Canine Parvovirus under 'Vaccination' on page 133).

Generally, a day without food, followed by a few days of small, frequent meals of a bland diet (such as cooked chicken or fish), or an appropriate prescription diet, should allow the stomach to settle. It is vital to ensure the patient is drinking and retaining sufficient water to cover losses resulting from the stomach upset in addition to the normal losses to be expected when healthy. Oral rehydration fluid may not be very appetising for the patient, in which case cooled boiled water should be offered. Fluids should initially be offered in small but frequent amounts to avoid over-drinking, which can result in further vomiting and thereby

dehydration and electrolyte imbalances. It is also important to wean the patient back on to routine food gradually or else another bout of gastritis may occur.

JOINT PROBLEMS
It is not unusual for older Bull Terriers to be stiff after exercise, particularly in cold weather. This is not really surprising, given that they are such busy dogs when young. This is such a game breed that a nine- or ten-year-old Bull Terrier will not readily forego an extra walk or take kindly to turning for home earlier than usual. Your veterinary surgeon will be able to advise you on ways of helping your dog cope with stiffness, not least of which will be to ensure that he is not overweight. Arthritic joints do not need to be burdened with extra bodyweight!

Regular exercise and a well-balanced diet should ensure that your Bull Terrier remains fit and healthy.
Alice van Kempen

LUMPS

Regularly handling and stroking your dog will enable the early detection of lumps and bumps. These may be due to infection (abscess), bruising, multiplication of particular cells from within the body, or even an external parasite (tick). If you are worried about any lump you find, have it checked by a veterinary surgeon.

OBESITY

Being overweight does predispose to many other problems, such as diabetes mellitus, heart disease and joint problems. It is so easily prevented by simply acting as your Bull Terrier's conscience. Ignore pleading eyes and feed according to your dog's waistline. The body condition is what matters qualitatively, alongside monitoring that individual's bodyweight as a quantitative measure. The Bull Terrier should,

in my opinion as a health professional, have at least a suggestion of a waist and it should be possible to feel the ribs beneath only a slight layer of fat.

Neutering does not automatically mean that your Bull Terrier will be overweight. Having an ovario-hysterectomy does slow down the body's rate of working, castration to a lesser extent, but it therefore means that your dog needs less food. I recommend cutting back a little on the amount of food fed a few weeks before neutering to accustom your Bull Terrier to less food. If she looks a little underweight on the morning of the operation, it will help the veterinary surgeon as well as giving her a little leeway weight-wise afterwards. It is always harder to lose weight after neutering than before, because of this slowing in the body's inherent metabolic rate.

TEETH

Eating food starts with the canine teeth gripping and killing prey in the wild, incisor teeth biting off pieces of food and the molar teeth chewing it. To be able to eat is vital for life, yet the actual health of the teeth is often overlooked: unhealthy teeth can predispose to disease, and not just by reducing the ability to eat. The presence of infection within the mouth can lead to bacteria entering the bloodstream and then filtering out at major organs, with the potential for serious consequences. That is not to forget that simply having dental pain can affect a dog's wellbeing, as anyone who has had toothache will confirm.

Veterinary dentistry has made huge leaps in recent years, so that it no longer consists of extraction as the treatment of necessity. Good dental health lies in the

hands of the owner, starting from the moment the dog comes into your care. Just as we have taken on responsibility for feeding, so we have acquired the task of maintaining good dental and oral hygiene. In an ideal world, we should brush our dogs' teeth as regularly as our own, but the Bull Terrier puppy who finds having his teeth brushed is a huge game and excuse to roll over and over on the ground requires loads of patience, twice a day.

There are alternative strategies, ranging from dental chewsticks to specially formulated foods, but the main thing is to be aware of your dog's mouth. At least train your puppy to permit full examination of his teeth. This will not only ensure you are checking in his mouth regularly but will also make your veterinary surgeon's job easier when there is a real need for your dog to 'open wide!'

INHERITED DISORDERS

Any individual, dog or human, may have an inherited disorder by virtue of the genes acquired from the parents. This is significant not only for the health of that individual but also because of the potential for transmitting the disorder on to that individual's offspring and to subsequent generations, depending on the mode of inheritance.

There are control schemes in place for some inherited disorders. In the US, for example, the Canine Eye Registration Foundation (CERF) was set up by dog breeders concerned about heritable eye disease, and provides a database of dogs who have been examined by diplomates of the American College of Veterinary Ophthalmologists.

To date, only a few conditions have been confirmed in the Bull Terrier as being hereditary. In alphabetical order, these include:

AORTIC STENOSIS
The affected individual is born

with a narrowing of the aorta, the main vessel leading away from the heart to supply blood around the body and to the head. The resultant turbulence in blood can be heard as a murmur with a stethoscope, but the presence of a murmur does not necessarily mean that an individual will go on to develop heart failure.

ENTROPION

This is an inrolling of the eyelids. There are degrees of entropion, ranging from a slight inrolling to the more serious case, requiring surgical correction because of the pain and damage to the surface of the eyeball.

FAMILIAL KIDNEY DISEASE (HEREDITARY NEPHRITIS)

Early detection of abnormal amounts of protein in the urine can be a pointer to this disease, with kidney failure developing from early adulthood onwards. All breeding stock, males and females, should be tested for signs of kidney disease using a straightforward urine test. The ratio of protein to creatinine in the urine should be less than 0.3. The test report may indicate that a ratio of 1.0 is satisfactory, but research indicates that, for Bull Terriers, a ratio greater than 0.3 (not caused by other factors such as an infection) indicates the onset of nephritis.

LETHAL ACRODERMATITIS

This is caused by an inherited defect in zinc metabolism, which results in death or euthanasia before reaching adulthood

CONGENITAL DEAFNESS

Classically associated with the white Bull Terrier, it is now recognised as occurring in coloured individuals as well, albeit at a lower rate. Deafness can occur in one or both ears. A unilaterally deaf Bull Terrier can hear in one ear only, which means he knows that you are calling him but is unable to locate your position. So he will scan until he finds you visually. This problem used to be called directional deafness. It is now possible to accurately assess a puppy's hearing from the age of five weeks, using the Brainstem Auditory Evoked Response test.

because of intractable infections and wasting. At a post-mortem examination, the thymus gland cannot be found or is smaller than usual.

It usually manifests before weaning. Affected pups have a lighter coat colour, their growth is stunted, and their feet splay, with the footpads and skin between the digits becoming red, cracked and crusty. There are also changes to the skin of the ears and around the mouth and eyes. Diarrhoea, pneumonia and more generalised skin infections develop.

Sadly, this condition does not respond to zinc supplementation.

MITRAL VALVE DYSPLASIA (MVD)

This is a congenital heart defect. An affected individual is born with a malformed heart valve between the two chambers of the left side of the heart. The heart's ability to act as a pump depends

on the integrity of its valves. A wide spectrum of effect is seen, ranging from a slight malformation, having little effect on life span, across to such a leaky valve that congestive heart failure develops while young.

Blood leaking back through the valve causes turbulence in the blood flow, and the normally clear click as the valve closes is muffled. This is heard as a murmur when a stethoscope is placed on the chest wall, especially over the valve, so that a common time to first suspect MVD is when a veterinary surgeon examines the puppy as a first health check or prior to starting a vaccination course. A detailed ultrasound examination is needed to diagnose and gauge the extent of the problem.

MVD and other heart defects may be so minor during puppyhood that they escape detection but then deteriorate progressively with age. So it is

It is now widely acknowledged that complementary therapies have a significant part to play in the treatment of animals. *Alice van Kempen.*

POLYCYSTIC KIDNEY DISEASE (PKD)

As well as resulting in early-onset kidney failure, there may be an abnormal thickening of heart valves as well, which results in heart failure. PKD can be diagnosed by an ultrasound scan of the kidneys. Sadly, the long-term outlook is poor. The origins of PKD in Bull Terriers can be traced to a single, widely used stud dog in Australia. The general population is believed to be free of this disease.

SKIN CONDITIONS

There are a number of skin disorders that may have an hereditary basis, especially where there may be an underlying allergy, which is often seasonal. Effects range from recurrent skin infections to compulsive licking of the paws (apparent as the classic pink discoloration of the fur) and incessant itchiness. There is also a zinc-responsive dermatosis found in pups fed a zinc-deficient diet – note that this is distinct from lethal acrodermatitis (see above).

COMPLEMENTARY THERAPIES

Just as for human health, I do believe that there is a place for alternative therapies alongside and complementing orthodox treatment under the supervision of a veterinary surgeon. That is why 'complementary therapies' is a better name.

Because animals do not have a choice, there are measures in place to safeguard their wellbeing

important for your veterinarian to listen to your Bull Terrier's heart during his annual check-up.

PATELLAR LUXATION

This is the condition that I point out to my children when I spot a dog walking along the road, giving a little hop for a few steps every now and again. The kneecap or patella is slipping out of position, locking the knee or stifle so that it will not bend, causing the characteristic hopping steps until the patella slips back into its position over the stifle joint. Surgical correction is possible in severely affected dogs, but many simply carry on intermittently hopping, the long-term effect inevitably being arthritis of the stifle.

and welfare. All manipulative treatment must be under the direction of a veterinary surgeon who has examined the patient and diagnosed the condition that he or she feels needs that form of treatment. This covers physiotherapy, chiropractic, osteopathy and swimming therapy. For example, dogs with arthritis who cannot exercise as freely as they were accustomed will enjoy the sensation of controlled non-weight-bearing exercise in water, and will benefit with improved muscling and overall fitness.

All other complementary therapies such as acupuncture, homoeopathy and aromatherapy, can only be carried out by veterinary surgeons who have been trained in that particular field. Acupuncture is mainly used in dogs for pain relief, often to good effect. The needles look more alarming to the owner, but they are very fine and are well tolerated by most canine patients. Speaking personally, superficial needling is not unpleasant and does help with pain relief.

Homoeopathy has had a mixed press in recent years. It is based on the concept of treating like with like. Additionally, a homoeopathic remedy is said to become more powerful the more it is diluted.

SUMMARY

As the owner of a Bull Terrier, you are responsible for his care and health. Not only must you make decisions on his behalf, you are also responsible for establishing a

With good care and management, your Bull Terrier should live a long, happy and healthy life. *Alice van Kempen*

lifestyle for him that will ensure he leads a long and happy life. Diet plays as important a part in this, as does exercise.

For the domestic dog, it is only in recent years that the need has been recognised for changing the diet to suit the dog as he grows, matures and then enters his twilight years. So-called life-stage diets try to match the nutritional needs of the dog as he progresses through life.

An adult dog food will suit the Bull Terrier living a standard family life. There are also foods for those Bull Terriers tactfully termed as obese-prone, such as those who have been neutered or are less active than others, or simply like their food. Do remember, though, that ultimately you are in control of your Bull Terrier's diet,

unless he is able to profit from scavenging!

On the other hand, prescription diets are of necessity fed under the supervision of a veterinary surgeon because each is formulated to meet the very specific needs of particular health conditions. Should a prescription diet be fed to a healthy dog, or to a dog with a different illness, there could be adverse effects.

It is important to remember that your Bull Terrier has no choice. As his owner, you are responsible for any decision made, so it must be as informed a decision as possible. Always speak to your vet if you have any worries about your Bully. He is not just a dog; from the moment you brought him home, he became a member of the family.

THE CONTRIBUTORS

THE EDITOR
DAVID HARRIS (BRUMMAGEM)

Dr. David Harris was raised in Birmingham, the home of James Hinks and the birthplace of the Bull Terrier. Involved with dogs since childhood, he has owned, bred and exhibited Bull Terriers since 1970 under the Brummagem affix. (Brummagem means something like the original Bull Terrier – made in Birmingham, or a cheap and flashy trinket. Take your pick.).

A recognised authority on the history and development of the Bull Terriers and indeed on the breed in general, David is an avid canine chronicler. His books – *Full Circle: A History of the Coloured Bull Terrier* (1989) and *Bull Terriers Today* (1998) – are viewed as classics within the fancy. David has written numerous breed articles for bulletins and magazines around the world. His most recent publication – *The Bully Breeds* (2008) – reviews the bull-and-terriers from Bullies and Staffords to Bostons and Pit Bulls.

A popular judge, David's travels have taken him around the world for more than 25 years – from Australia and New Zealand to continental Europe and the UK and from South Africa and South America to Canada and, of course, all around the USA.

A long time member of the Bull Terrier Club of America, David has fulfilled many roles – from president to chairperson of the health committee. He is the recipient of the Club's Bar Sinister award for extreme service the breed.

Since 1979 David has lived with his Bullies in the high desert of New Mexico, where he is on the faculty of the University of New Mexico.
See Chapter Two: The first Bull Terriers and Chapter Seven: The Perfect Bull Terrier.

EILEEN FOY (BYLEY)
Eileen started showing Kerry Blue Terriers in 1970 and began awarding CCs in 1975. In 1977 she married Brian Foy of Foyri Bull Terriers and both kennels have flourished since then, winning many shows and producing several Group winners.

Today Eileen awards CCs in several terrier breeds in the UK as well as in Ireland, Finland, South Africa, Denmark and Russia.

Eileen has served on the committees of several terrier clubs, including the Miniature Bull Terrier Club, for which she produced their first handbook. Eileen's canine publications continue to grow and she is currently working on a book about grooming. She has also lectured extensively on animal care.
See Chapter One: Getting to Know the Bull Terrier.

MOLLY WEEKS (ROSALYN)
Molly Weeks has had a long, prestigious career in the arts. Specialising in drama and theatre arts, she has also had a lot of involvement with radio and broadcasting.

Her commitment to the dog world mirrors her media achievements. As well as being the author of several books about Bull Terriers, Molly is very active in promoting animal welfare issues and responsible dog ownership. She is a Fellow of the Sir Winston Churchill Memorial Trust, researching the role of education in animal welfare and she is the Chairman of the Hornsea Dog Owner's Club. She was Secretary of the Bull Terrier Club for 13 years and is currently Chairman of the Coloured Bull Terrier Club.
See Chapter Three: A Bull Terrier for your Lifestyle and Chapter Four: The New Arrival.

DAWN GODSALL (NEVERLAND)
As a child, Dawn was 'dog mad' and as a child would walk neighbours' dogs many a mile. She got her first dog aged 12, a lovely crossbred called Andy who she used to take to local exemption shows on the bus.

Building on her love of dogs, Dawn's first job on leaving school was working for Miss May Tovey of the Yevot Japanese Spaniels and Chihuahua, but she had a soft spot for Bull Terriers even at this stage and used to avidly read Mr Oppenheimer's breed notes in the dog paper every week.

Dawn bought her first Bull Terrier, Jessica, in 1987, from Brian Foy. Dawn and her husband quickly became smitten with the white bitch they had acquired and the breed in general.

Dawn bred a couple of litters from Jessica and started to compete in shows, which sparked a lifelong interest. Dawn has since bred three Champions, two whites and a coloured. The coloured Bull Terrier is very close to Dawn's heart.

Dawn is a show judge and is involved on the committee of two Bull Terrier clubs. She also edits the CBTC Bulletin.
See Chapter Five: The Best of Care.

JULIA BARNES
Julia has owned and trained a number of different dog breeds, and is a puppy socialiser for Dogs for the Disabled. A former journalist, she has written many books, including several on dog training and behaviour. Julia is indebted to Juliet Shaw (Badlesmere) for her specialist knowledge of Bull Terriers.
See Chapter Six: Training and Socialisation

JULIET SHAW (BADLESMERE)
Juliet's first Bull Terrier was a seven-year-old rescue. Thereafter she slowly but surely got sucked in to the world of Bull Terriers, showing, breeding and judging.

Juliet is a worldwide judge and she is also involved in Bull Terrier Rescue and re-habilitation. Juliet owns two 'welfares', both with sad stories before they were adopted.

Today, Juliet breeds Bull Terriers and Mini Bull Terriers, with great emphasis on health and natural feeding. The Minis are highly successful in the show ring and in great demand from older people no longer able to cope with a large, powerful dog.

Juliet's mentor was Miss Eva Weatherill of the famous Ormandy/ Souperlative Kennels, and Juliet strives to breed to her exacting standards, as well as freely offering advice to anyone having problems with their Bull Terriers.

ALISON LOGAN MA VetMB MRCVS
Alison qualified as a veterinary surgeon from Cambridge University in 1989, having been brought up surrounded by all manner of animals and birds in the north Essex countryside. She has been in practice in her home town ever since, living with her husband, two children and Labrador Retriever Pippin.

She contributes on a regular basis to *Veterinary Times, Veterinary Nurse Times, Dogs Today, Cat World* and *Pet Patter*, the PetPlan newsletter. In 1995, Alison won the Univet Literary Award with an article on Cushing's Disease, and she won it again (as the Vetoquinol Literary Award) in 2002, writing about common conditions in the Shar-Pei.
See Chapter Eight: Happy and Healthy.

USEFUL ADDRESSES

KENNEL & BREED CLUBS

UK
The Kennel Club
1 Clarges Street, London, W1J 8AB
Tel: 0870 606 6750
Fax: 0207 518 1058
Web: www.the-kennel-club.org.uk

To obtain up-to-date contact information for the following breed clubs, please contact the Kennel Club:
- Bull Terrier Club
- Bull Terrier Club of Wales
- Coloured Bull Terrier Club
- East Anglian Bull Terrier Club
- Miniature Bull Terrier Club
- North East Bull Terrier Club
- Northern Provincial Bull Terrier Club
- Notts and Derby District Bull Terrier Club
- Scottish Bull Terrier Club
- South Eastern Counties Bull Terrier Club
- Ulster Bull Terrier Club
- West of England Bull Terrier Club
- Yorkshire Bull Terrier Club

USA
American Kennel Club (AKC)
5580 Centerview Drive,
Raleigh, NC 27606, USA.
Tel: 919 233 9767
Fax: 919 233 3627
Email: info@akc.org
Web: www.akc.org

United Kennel Club (UKC)
100 E Kilgore Rd, Kalamazoo,
MI 49002-5584, USA.
Tel: 269 343 9020
Fax: 269 343 7037
Web:www.ukcdogs.com/

Bull Terrier Club of America
www.btca.com/

For contact details of regional clubs, please contact the Bull Terrier Club of America.

AUSTRALIA
Australian National Kennel Council (ANKC)
The Australian National Kennel Council is the administrative body for pure breed canine affairs in Australia. It does not, however, deal directly with dog exhibitors, breeders or judges. For information pertaining to breeders, clubs or shows, please contact the relevant State or Territory Controlling Body.

Dogs Australian Capital Teritory
PO Box 815, Dickson ACT 2602
Tel: (02) 6241 4404
Fax: (02) 6241 1129
Email: administrator@dogsact.org.au
Web: www.dogsact.org.au

Dogs New South Wales
PO Box 632, St Marys, NSW 1790
Tel: (02) 9834 3022 or 1300 728 022 (NSW Only)
Fax: (02) 9834 3872
Email: info@dogsnsw.org.au
Web: www.dogsnsw.org.au

Dogs Northern Territory
PO Box 37521, Winnellie NT 0821
Tel: (08) 8984 3570
Fax: (08) 8984 3409
Email: admin@dogsnt.com.au
Web: www.dogsnt.com.au

Dogs Queensland
PO Box 495, Fortitude Valley Qld 4006
Tel: (07) 3252 2661
Fax: (07) 3252 3864
Email: info@dogsqueensland.org.au
Web: www.dogsqueensland.org.au

Dogs South Australia
PO Box 844
Prospect East SA 5082
Tel: (08) 8349 4797
Fax: (08) 8262 5751
Email: info@dogssa.com.au
Web: www.dogssa.com.au

Tasmanian Canine Association Inc
The Rothman Building
PO Box 116
Glenorchy Tas 7010
Tel: (03) 6272 9443
Fax: (03) 6273 0844
Email: tca@iprimus.com.au
Web: www.tasdogs.com

Dogs Victoria
Locked Bag K9
Cranbourne VIC 3977
Tel: (03)9788 2500
Fax: (03) 9788 2599
Email: office@dogsvictoria.org.au
Web: www.dogsvictoria.org.au

Dogs Western Australia
PO Box 1404
Canning Vale WA 6970
Tel: (08) 9455 1188
Fax: (08) 9455 1190
Email: k9@dogswest.com
Web: www.dogswest.com

INTERNATIONAL
Fédération Cynologique Internationalé (FCI)/World Canine Organisation
Place Albert 1er, 13, B-6530 Thuin,
Belgium.
Tel: +32 71 59.12.38
Fax: +32 71 59.22.29
Web: www.fci.be/

TRAINING AND BEHAVIOUR

UK
Association of Pet Dog Trainers
PO Box 17, Kempsford, GL7 4WZ
Telephone: 01285 810811
Email: APDToffice@aol.com
Web: http://www.apdt.co.uk

Association of Pet Behaviour Counsellors
PO BOX 46, Worcester, WR8 9YS
Telephone: 01386 751151
Fax: 01386 750743
Email: info@apbc.org.uk
Web: http://www.apbc.org.uk/

USA
Association of Pet Dog Trainers
101 North Main Street, Suite 610
Greenville, SC 29601, USA.
Tel: 1 800 738 3647
Email: information@apdt.com
Web: www.apdt.com/

American College of Veterinary Behaviorists
College of Veterinary Medicine, 4474 Tamu,
Texas A&M University
College Station, Texas 77843-4474
Web: http://dacvb.org/

American Veterinary Society of Animal Behavior
Web: www.avsabonline.org/

AUSTRALIA

APDT Australia Inc
PO Box 3122, Bankstown Square, NSW 2200, Australia.
Email: secretary@apdt.com.au
Web: www.apdt.com.au

Canine Behaviour
For details of regional behvaiourists, contact the relevant State/Territory Controlling Body.

ACTIVITIES

UK
Agility Club
http://www.agilityclub.co.uk/

British Flyball Association
PO Box 990, Doncaster, DN1 9FY
Telephone: 01628 829623
Email: secretary@flyball.org.uk
Web: http://www.flyball.org.uk/

USA
North American Dog Agility Council
P.O. Box 1206, Colbert,
OK 74733, USA.
Web: www.nadac.com/

North American Flyball Association, Inc.
1333 West Devon Avenue, #512
Chicago, IL 60660
Tel/Fax: 800 318 6312
Email: flyball@flyball.org
Web: www.flyball.org/

AUSTRALIA
Agility Dog Association of Australia
ADAA Secretary, PO Box 2212,
Gailes, QLD 4300, Australia.
Tel: 0423 138 914
Email: admin@adaa.com.au
Web: www.adaa.com.au/

NADAC Australia (North American Dog Agility Council - Australian Division)
12 Wellman Street, Box Hill South, Victoria 3128, Australia.
Email: shirlene@nadacaustralia.com
Web: www.nadacaustralia.com/

Australian Flyball Association
PO Box 4179, Pitt Town, NSW 2756
Tel: 0407 337 939
Email: info@flyball.org.au
Web: www.flyball.org.au/

INTERNATIONAL

World Canine Freestyle Organisation
P.O. Box 350122, Brooklyn, NY 11235-2525, USA
Tel: (718) 332-8336
Fax: (718) 646-2686
Email: wcfodogs@aol.com
Web: www.worldcaninefreestyle.org

HEALTH

UK
Alternative Veterinary Medicine Centre
Chinham House, Stanford in the Vale,
Oxfordshire, SN7 8NQ
Tel: 01367 710324
Fax: 01367 718243
Web: www.alternativevet.org/

British Small Animal Veterinary Association
Woodrow House, 1 Telford Way,
Waterwells Business Park, Quedgeley,
Gloucestershire, GL2 2AB
Tel: 01452 726700
Fax: 01452 726701
Email: customerservices@bsava.com
Web: http://www.bsava.com/

Royal College of Veterinary Surgeons
Belgravia House, 62-64 Horseferry Road,
London, SW1P 2AF
Tel: 0207 222 2001
Fax: 0207 222 2004
Email: admin@rcvs.org.uk
Web: www.rcvs.org.uk

USA
American Holistic Veterinary Medical Association
2218 Old Emmorton Road
Bel Air, MD 21015
Tel: 410 569 0795
Fax 410 569 2346
Email: office@ahvma.org
Web: www.ahvma.org/

American Veterinary Medical Association
1931 North Meacham Road, Suite 100,
Schaumburg, IL 60173-4360, USA.
Tel: 800 248 2862
Fax: 847 925 1329
Web: www.avma.org

American College of Veterinary Surgeons
19785 Crystal Rock Dr, Suite 305
Germantown, MD 20874, USA.
Tel: 301 916 0200
Toll Free: 877 217 2287
Fax: 301 916 2287
Email: acvs@acvs.org
Web: www.acvs.org/

AUSTRALIA
Australian Holistic Vets
Web: www.ahv.com.au/

Australian Small Animal Veterinary Association
40/6 Herbert Street, St Leonards, NSW 2065, Australia.
Tel: 02 9431 5090
Fax: 02 9437 9068
Email: asava@ava.com.au
Web: www.asava.com.au

Australian Veterinary Association
Unit 40, 6 Herbert Street, St Leonards,
NSW 2065, Australia.
Tel: 02 9431 5000
Fax: 02 9437 9068
Web: www.ava.com.au

Australian College Veterinary Scientists
Building 3, Garden City Office Park,
2404 Logan Road, Eight Mile Plains,
Queensland 4113, Australia.
Tel: 07 3423 2016
Fax: 07 3423 2977
Email: admin@acvs.org.au
Web: http://acvsc.org.au

ASSISTANCE DOGS

Canine Partners
Mill Lane, Heyshott, Midhurst,
, GU29 0ED
Tel: 08456 580480
Fax: 08456 580481
Web: www.caninepartners.co.uk

Dogs for the Disabled
The Frances Hay Centre, Blacklocks Hill,
Banbury, Oxon, OX17 2BS
Tel: 01295 252600
Web: www.dogsforthedisabled.org

Guide Dogs for the Blind Association
Burghfield Common, Reading, RG7 3YG
Tel: 01189 835555
Fax: 01189 835433
Web: www.guidedogs.org.uk/

Hearing Dogs for Deaf People
The Grange, Wycombe Road, Saunderton,
Princes Risborough, Bucks, HP27 9NS
Tel: 01844 348100
Fax: 01844 348101
Web: www.hearingdogs.org.uk

Pets as Therapy
14a High Street, Wendover, Aylesbury,
Bucks. HP22 6EA.
Tel: 01845 345445
Fax: 01845 550236
Web: http://www.petsastherapy.org/

Support Dogs
21 Jessops Riverside, Brightside Lane,
Sheffield, S9 2RX
Tel: 01142 617800
Fax: 01142 617555
Email: supportdogs@btconnect.com
Web: www.support-dogs.org.uk

USA
Therapy Dogs International
88 Bartley Road, Flanders, NJ 07836,.
Tel: 973 252 9800
Fax: 973 252 7171
Email: tdi@gti.net
Web: www.tdi-dog.o

Therapy Dogs Inc.
P.O. Box 20227, Cheyenne, WY 82003.
Tel: 307 432 0272.
Fax: 307-638-2079
Web: www.therapydogs.com

Delta Society - Pet Partners
875 124th Ave NE, Suite 101 • Bellevue,
WA 98005 USA.
Email: info@DeltaSociety.org
Web: www.deltasociety.org

Comfort Caring Canines
8135 Lare Street, Philadelphia, PA 19128.
Email: ccc@comfortcaringcanines.org
Web: www.comfortcaringcanines.org/

AUSTRALIA
AWARE Dogs Australia, Inc
PO Box 883, Kuranda, Queensland, 488,
Australia.
Tel: 07 4093 8152
Web: www.awaredogs.org.au/

Delta Society — Therapy Dogs
Web: www.deltasociety.com.au